Alan

Thank you for all
your encouragement &
support

Mark

# Ring a Ding Ding

*First Edition published 2019 by*

2QT Limited (Publishing)

Settle, North Yorkshire BD24 9RH United Kingdom

Copyright © Mark Fuller 2019

The right of Mark Fuller to be identified as the author of this work has been asserted by him/her in accordance with the Copyright, Designs and Patents Act 1988

Publisher Disclaimer:

The events in this memoir are described according to the Authors recollection; recognition and understanding of the events and individuals mentioned and are in no way intended to mislead or offend. As such the Publisher does not hold any responsibility for any inaccuracies or opinions expressed by the author. Every effort has been made to acknowledge and gain any permission from organisations and persons mentioned in this book. Any enquiries should be directed to the author.

Cover Design by Charlotte Mouncey

Printed in Great Britain by Latitude Press

A CIP catalogue record for this book is available from the British Library

ISBN - 978-1-913071-36-3

Mark has laid out, physically and mentally, his and Lucy's big adventure of buying and managing an inn, in an erudite, revealing, helpful and humorous way. The trials and tribulations are delivered with levity and wit; the commercial aspects in an informative way. You will enjoy reading about their dealings with "the great and the good" and the "hoi polloi".

John Anthony Helliwell
Chevalier de l' Ordre des Arts et des Lettres
Saxophonist of *Supertramp*

# Ring a Ding Ding

## THE MAKING OF 5-STAR INN

# MARK FULLER

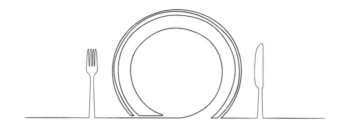

# Acknowledgements

Thank you to all the great staff who worked with us throughout the eleven years, there are many who I haven't mentioned by name but every single person is remembered and appreciated for their contribution to the Sun Inn.

My wife Lucy, for all her patience with me as I wrote this book, during the eleven years of running the inn and fourteen years and counting of happy marriage

Allan Tunningley for helping me in writing and preparing the book for publishing

Lynda Skinner for her encouragement and support

Moore and Smalley support in the production of the book

Iain and Jenny Black for allowing the use of past photos, logos and sharing past memories of the way we ran our business

Lucy Barden Photography for some of the photos

My two lifelong mentors Terry Erard and Iain Gardiner, for having so much faith in me

And finally last but perhaps not the least or littlest, Eunice and Tony for their unending support and enthusiasm.

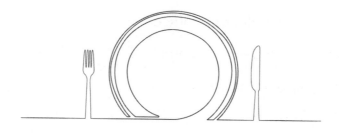

# Contents

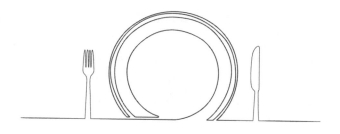

# Introduction

I often glided past David Skinner's table while he held court, assuming the role of Executive Landlord of the Sun Inn, to get his verdict on the Dover Sole that he would always order in advance. He would respond with 'extremely average' if he felt it was good and **'ring-a-ding-ding'** if it was **excellent**. Followed by: 'I will have another bottle of that Sancerre; do help yourself to a glass, old boy.' It seemed to sum up the complete joy he had for the licensed trade.

One of a host of real characters that made Kirkby Lonsdale special, David had had a very successful career in public houses in Liverpool. He knew all the tricks of the trade and just loved the whole dynamic of the business. He was a larger than life character; cheeky, caring and charismatic. He always said he could write a book about his experiences as a licensee, which he would recount in snippets and always with good humour over the years that he frequented the inn.

My one regret was that David never wrote that book before he passed away, so I thought I should not delay in sharing with you the ins and outs of such a life.

After my career in a stressful corporate hotel life, David taught me in his very own laid-back style how to relax and enjoy running your own hospitality business. He believed that to run a successful Pub / Inn you needed to be: 'a Diplomat', 'a Door Mat' and an 'Aristocrat'. He always acted the part of all three with great style.

This story is dedicated to Dave Skinner and sets out the 'ring-a-ding-ding' years that consumed Lucy's and my life while we owned the Sun Inn and all that was contained in running it, including at times being that Diplomat, Door Mat and Aristocrat!

Dave, thank you for giving me the inspiration to write this book of snippets. I look forward to joining you one day at the Inn of the next life for a well deserved pint of Landlord, or Landlady as you used to call it.

Dave in one of his Aristocratic poses

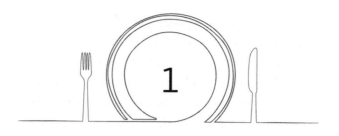

# Big Hairy Audacious Goal

Bells have been an enduring theme in my life. I was born within the sound of England's most famous examples: the Bow Bells of London. I have spent my working life in the hospitality sector where bells have traditionally rung out last orders for as long as anyone can remember, and now I am about to tell the story of the inn I ran with my wife Lucy, which for centuries has stood well within the ringing range of the bells of St Mary's Church in Kirkby Lonsdale. As I have already mentioned, it is at the Sun Inn that I also encountered the ring-a-ding-ding catchphrase of our most treasured customer, Dave Skinner. So you can see that bells have been a constant campanological companion of mine.

But they have not always heralded good news.

This is a story of many challenges, a number of which were linked with the charm of the church bells as well as the sadness and alarm they bring. All these challenges we would have to rise to if we were to make a success of our fledgling business and achieve our BHAG.

Ah, yes – the BHAG.

This odd acronym was first firmly planted in my mind during a business conference one fresh summer's morning in Cheshire. To many, the Big Hairy Audacious Goal might sound like the title of a fantasy movie straight out of Hollywood, but it was a concept firmly grounded in reality and one which would ultimately help me fulfil a long-held personal ambition.

It was back in the Noughties when I was introduced to the BHAG by Carl Lever, a relatively young chief executive at the De Vere group, the company I worked for as a hotel general manager. He highlighted the acronym during a two-day corporate conference entitled Shine, which was held back in 2005 as part of one of those change programmes businesses need to go through from time to time.

Well, Carl certainly shone a light as he proceeded to turn what some might consider a dry subject – Return on capital investment in the hotel trade – into something quite inspirational.

For me, and probably for a few of the other people in the room, it was the first time anyone had properly explained the full ins and outs of the return on capital investment in the hotel business. This was the missing part of my financial experience in the corporate world to date – and it was one that should have perhaps been the first.

Previously, all the emphasis was about maximising net profit: concentrating on margins, conversions, growths, market penetration and percentages in order to achieve profit growth.

The conference's significance would soon extend beyond financial insights. When I sat down at 11.30am for that second session – Imagining is believing – I had no idea I was about to make a transformational decision.

Believing is the most important aspect of making things happen and we were asked by Carl to imagine something company-business related that we had always wanted to achieve – our very own Big Hairy Audacious Goal, if you like – and to dwell on it for a short while.

This really caught my attention as my dreams, wishes and audacious goals were at the time wrapped up in my own potential purchase of a run-down pub in the historic market town of Kirkby Lonsdale.

For the next ten minutes, I allowed myself to drift away from the corporate world and dwell on something I'd always so badly wanted, but due to money, timing, child commitments and, I suspect, my own wavering belief, had not been previously possible.

Those minutes of reflection, in that second session of a corporate conference one bright summer's day in Cheshire, were to prove pivotal – inspiring me to really believe I could achieve a dream. But by now it was not my dream alone: I was to be sharing this remarkable, and scary, journey with my co-pilot, wife, business partner and best friend in the world, Lucy.

Our quest would not be easy; really worthwhile challenges never are. The one we faced back in 2005 echoed an experience I had had four decades earlier when, in my late teens, I was pursuing success in the world of diving, and I was faced with performing a nerve-racking forward two-and-a-half somersault dive from the ten metre board.

I was a reasonably experienced diver and had trained up to it, but the dive was a big one from a very high board. And I had no choice but to master it if I was to be accepted as part of the Highgate Diving Club Show team for tours to Ireland and Canada.

Of course, you needed the skill to do the dive; but most importantly you needed belief that you could complete it without losing your nerve – what was colloquially and affectionately referred to by the diving fraternity as 'shit or bust!'.

Self-belief is always something I've battled with; but, on those occasions when I have taken the plunge, the 'dive' – whether into the pool or a new work challenge – was already completed in my mind well before I climbed those metaphorical steps to the top board to take my leap of faith.

The question from that two-day corporate conference in Cheshire back in 2005 was; could Lucy and I keep our nerve and achieve the same success with our dream inn?

In my mind, this was now answered.

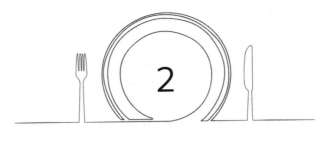

# Our Lives

I came into this world in late May 1956 at The Woolwich Memorial Hospital, Shooters Hill, London, the son of a vicar. The window of the ward had a panoramic view over London and the location was charmed with the **ring-a-ding-ding** of Bow Bells, granting me the birthright of a Cockney. May is a bright and optimistic month, with winter over and the beginning of the summer sun. I'm certain that this early bright and optimistic feeling rubbed off on me and helped cast the die of my personality that I retain today.

My family pet name was Markey Sparky. I quite liked the Sparky element but always thought Markey was a little babyish; looking back, it was probably apt as I always had a slightly timid and sensitive nature coupled with an interest in everything.

Being the youngest of three, the money ran out to send me to private school and, in retrospect, the money might have been wasted with my dyslexia and low boredom threshold. All I can say is that I attended school and thrived on sport. What I lacked for in adjectives, nouns, Pythagoras and logarithms, I made up for in eye, hand and leg co-ordination on the field and in the swimming pool.

After winning a Croydon schools' diving competition, I was put forward by the school to join a six-week springboard diving class run by Terry Erard.

Mark performing a back dive from a one meter springboard at
Ironmonger Row swimming baths, London

It's this encounter that changed my life. Terry took me on along with
four others to be part of his diving squad. Aged eleven, we trained five
days a week for four hours each day after school and at weekends, which

took me way out of my comfort zone. Learning somersaults and twists in mid-air and diving forward, backwards, inwards and reverse-ways of a range of one, three and five-metre boards tested my timidity at each stage; but my desire and imagination were spurred on by being among national and international divers, and a whole new world of confidence, strength, agility and optimism opened up for me.

When I was sixteen, my parents moved to Manchester, a triumph for my education and a disaster for my diving. Five O Levels and one A Level were enough to get me back down to London to Westminster College Hotel School and a return to diving, this time with a new coach, Mick Cannon, an international diver and diving coach. For three years, the battle of a career in diving or a career in hotels was fought. Hotels won.

My sport gave me the discipline and drive for success in the hospitality business and a life-long friendship and mentoring by my former coach Terry and the understanding of what it takes to be an international diver from Mick. What's quite amazing is that back then coaching was provided freely and was mainly done for the love of the sport and the desire to help like-minded people to succeed. That generosity has never been lost on me; it always gives me such pleasure to help others in business or life. It's a constant reminder of my good fortune, being a boy with never any money or the knowledge to make success.

My hospitality career really took off with Forte and then with Moat House Hotels, and in between this demanding time I married and my then wife Cheryl produced and nurtured four lovely children, two boys and two girls. Sadly this ended in divorce, with all the hurt and upset that goes with it.

Following the painful time of my divorce, I felt the need to move on, and when a general manager's position became available at Chester Moat House, I applied. I was offered the job and accepted it before I had even visited the property. A reckless move, perhaps, but I had faith in my boss Iain Gardiner with whom I had worked closely before, and anyway I really needed a fresh new start.

The brief I was given was firm and straight to the point: 'Mark,' Iain said with laconic candour, 'this is a sort-out job!'

He was not wrong.

The Chester hotel was a cash cow with high occupancies, yet it had a tired feel and needed a new injection of life, both in the product and people delivering it, to head off significant new hospitality competition in nearby Liverpool where they were opening smart 4-star hotels, fast.

I spent my first two days clearing out years of files, old paperwork and assorted rubbish from the general manager's office, leaving only the profit and loss accounts and staff records. Then I instructed the maintenance department to decorate, carpet and fit out the office with three new sofas, signifying to all a very different approach and style. This new environment would allow key members of the team to discuss how we were going to change this business in a relaxed and informal setting. I believed it would help us communicate as equals and win over hearts and minds for the task ahead.

These sofas also provided just the right setting for hotel clients who were considering placing large contracts of business into the hotel. Before any show round I would always invite them into my office and get a chance to know them and most importantly establish their full requirements, including their likes, dislikes and the things that were important to them, before any show round was to commence. Following the show round the office was just the right place to close the sale.

A case in point was when the then Deputy Prime Minister, John Prescott (now Lord Prescott) was planning to hold a European Conference in the hotel and in various parts of the city of Chester. He came up from London with his entourage and my three sofas stood up well to his tabloid "Two Jags" image and they did their magic and we won the business.

Perhaps because of my divorce, or a mid-life crisis, now for the first time in my working career I felt liberated. I could be me, no longer in the strait-jacket of conformity; I was branching out and knew what I wanted. My job as general manager at Chester Moat House gave me the fresh impetus I desired. However, I had no idea at the time how my new role would also bring a wonderful fresh start to my personal life.

Lucy and I have contradictory recollections of our first meeting. As regional sales manager, she was one of a number of the company's executives invited into my new salubrious, three-sofa office for meetings. I say 'invited', but Lucy saw it quite differently, telling her colleagues afterwards that she felt she had been 'summoned'.

There are also contradictory recollections about her legs, with Lucy asking her colleagues to remind her to wear trousers and not a skirt the next time she visited the GM (General Manager) at Chester.

It's true, I did think at the time that Lucy had nice legs. But it was really her shoes I was interested in, because they seemed to say a lot about her. They were individual and stylish, definitely not from a chain store, soft and gentle, yet certainly strong enough to stand up to the hustle and bustle of work life. I thought that here was someone who was fun, clever and quietly confident both about herself and the world of hotel sales and I wanted her on my team, shoes and all.

Lucy was brought up with fresh wind and sunshine in her hair. She loved the Lido in her home town of Morecambe and, in her childhood, would spend whole days around the pool or combing the rock pools and sand dunes of the bay. A lively and bright girl, quick on her feet, happy to flirt with danger but safe with strong self-preservation strategies and tactics that kept her out of harm most of the time.

Like me, school did not get the best out of this bright lively lady. She left school at sixteen to do a two-year B-tech in hospitality and once her focus was channelled she went on to a four-year degree in hotel management that led to a career in hotel sales where she applied her bright and logical approach to great success ending up as Head of Sales Development for De Vere Hotels.

Her birth dad, who died when she was very young, was a chartered accountant and a love of numbers was obviously in her genes, too; but this remained dormant until activated in the world of hotel sales where she brought order and clarity from numbers to develop sales strategies and approaches to financial success.

Over a number of meetings and joint appointments with customers,

Lucy and I gradually grew closer, leading to the fateful night we first kissed. Again, Lucy has her own version of what happened in the early hours of that morning as we entertained some very drunk customers who were enjoying a familiarisation visit to the hotel. She says I lured her behind the bar to change the music on the pretext of creating a little party atmosphere and then took advantage of her while out of sight of our guests. All I know is that it was a kiss of such excitement and joy it sealed the closeness that had gradually built between us.

The romantic dates that inevitably followed were so special, they bonded us together and led eventually to Lucy moving into my little cottage. With Lucy by my side and the support of my boss Iain who, fortunately, laughed when he saw the sofas in the office, I felt confident and able to develop the hotel with new products and services. We also raised the hotel's profile in the local community and produced transformational profits which culminated in us winning the Hotel of the Year Award within the group.

By now in my mid-forties, I was hungry for more and the desire to run my own hospitality business was like raging hormones running through an adolescent, only slightly tempered by experience. There were two phrases I held dearly at this time; and funnily enough one came from my diving coach and mentor Terry Erard and the other from my work mentor and boss Iain Gardiner. They were: 'mark time' and 'strike when the iron is hot'. Although on the face of it these might be considered contradictory, they proved to be valuable guidance.

For during the next four years, Lucy and I did both.

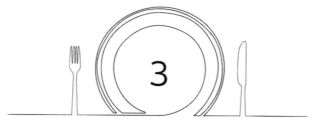

# Marking Time

I continued living with the unfired dream to run our own business by 'marking time', joining my latest hotel as General Manager, at the De Vere group's Daresbury Park Hotel at Warrington, where I learned a different corporate approach – including the need for that Big Hairy Audacious Goal.

A little later, it also transpired that Lucy needed a change, and she joined the same organisation in a senior role for the last year I was with them. We were obviously destined to be together in both home and in business.

By then I knew Lucy also shared my ambition to own and run a bed and breakfast-style hotel although, without one to buy, all we could do was work on various hospitality business models that we thought we might be able to afford. Finding the right place to put any of these models into practice would prove our first major challenge.

Over a period of three years, we spent time developing our cottage and garden in the village of Bretton in North Wales, just over the border from Chester, while also inspecting four potential hotel businesses, at Cheltenham, on the Wirral, in Macclesfield and at Haworth near Bradford, where the Bronte sisters lived. However, none of these really inspired us, despite our desperately trying to make a case for each one to work.

Then one year for my birthday, Lucy booked us an overnight stay at The Inn at Whitwell. We'd previously stumbled upon the inn while walking in the Trough of Bowland and called in for an enjoyable Sunday lunch. The place inspired us and triggered the vision which we instantly started working on and 'banked' in our minds: that of a 'destination inn', where the inn becomes just as much a destination as the village, town or other setting in which it is located.

Lucy and I loved the area and were contemplating moving to the Forest of Bowland while in our existing jobs. Areas like this and the Lune Valley are almost hijacked by their close proximity to the Lake District and the Yorkshire Dales that seem to get all the attention, yet they are equally, stunningly beautiful. The extra commute time from Chester would have been easily made up for the charm of rural life, log fires, local pub, long walks and taking in nature.

Yet, despite knowing more about what we wanted to achieve, and the sort of area we wanted to achieve it in, we still didn't have a business to make an offer on. But that was about to change, thanks to a quirk of fate involving cheese and a marriage proposal.

Choosing the right date and time and the conducive environment for a marriage proposal is one of the keys to a successful outcome, I thought. So Christmas Eve seemed to me a good time. We had the cottage all festively dressed, Christmas carols on low, the wood burner all aglow and the presents piled under the tree, including an extra-small one I had added. There were just the two of us. Supper was in the oven and a nice bottle of red wine open and the evening was ours. Lucy and I had agreed to open presents on Christmas Eve, because I always worked on Christmas Day.

Lucy had spotted the extra-small present put beside the tree that day and was intrigued but had not guessed the contents nor did she want to bring it to my attention, but had decided to open this one last.

We were full of excitement and joy and really happy with all our presents to each other and from family when it came to the final mystery present disguised as a Christmas present. Fortunately, the jeweller from whom I bought the ring mentioned that if it did not work out I could take it back. I assured him there would be no need for that, although just at this moment it did flash through my mind, what it would be like having to return such an item. I would have to wait until no other customers were present and quietly admit my failure.

As Lucy opened the wrapper, you could see her think, 'Jewellery, lovely', then, 'a ring – oh my goodness!' Both our heartbeats jumped a gear and the words just flowed. Then silence. For a surprised lady, it took a few more moments for Lucy to compose her response. We can both safely say that there has not been a Christmas more special than this. Lucy did not have to say anything, but in her moment of silence you could see the answer in her eyes.

Our wedding day in 2005 was to be 27th May – deliberately chosen by me two days after my birthday which, I hoped, would mean I could never forget our anniversary. By the beginning of April, we were in the full throes of organising the nuptials. To add an extra dimension to the reception, we decided that as well as a wedding cake we ought to have a cheesecake for our guests to enjoy. Luckily, Lucy knew that a former work colleague and friend Jules along with her husband, self-confessed cheese fanatic John Natlacen, had just opened a shop in Kirkby Lonsdale called Churchmouse Cheese. So we ordered from them an amazing cheesecake that would consist of a pyramid of truckles of cheese, all decorated with figs and fruit. We weren't to know then how much of a catalyst this decision would be.

In an amazing coincidence, Lucy had already come across the particulars of a Kirkby Lonsdale pub called the Sun Inn while trawling through agents' websites looking for businesses for sale; but it was the link with cheese that really prompted us to visit the town to check out the property, which just happened to be next door to the Churchmouse shop. Perhaps it was more fate than coincidence that we ended up as neighbours to John and Jules, who would go on to be valuable business associates as well as close friends, helping us to achieve our dream.

After our initial viewing of the Sun Inn, however, we realised it wouldn't be an easy business to take on. The pub, which looked very sorry for itself, was owned by a pub company and run like a hostelry that had seen better days. The UK smoking ban hadn't come into force at this time and nicotine seemed to drip from the ceiling and walls. A number of guest bedrooms were occupied by live-in staff and they resembled teenager bedrooms from hell. The chefs had a poster of a large naked lady on the kitchen wall and the floors everywhere were sticky with beer, gum and grease.

Everything was wrong, apart from the charm of the seventeenth-century building and the potential of the bedroom stock. Yet it struck us as a perfect opportunity, the type of 'destination inn' we had envisioned after seeing the Inn at Whitewell. But then we stood back and said something like: 'Why on earth would we want to take this on?'

The Sun Inn was a major project and a daunting task to embark on with none of the corporate support we were used to. Even so, our interest was sufficiently aroused to jump to the next stage.

The inn was on the market for £650K, but it was clear from the financial statement that this price was over-valuing its current earnings potential. With water coming through the roof in parts, we were uncertain whether it reflected the bricks and mortar price either.

After a couple of days spent number-crunching and reflecting on the theoretical business models we'd looked at previously, we came up with a price of £605K subject to survey. We submitted this to the selling agent, who made us feel as if we had not made a serious offer and were a waste of time. Nevertheless, the offer was put to the vendors for consideration and we set about organising a survey and valuation.

Despite our £605K offer being initially treated almost dismissively, it was eventually accepted and so we went ahead with the survey. This cost £1,800 – a lot of money to us then, especially if for whatever reason we didn't go ahead. The report came in quickly, only for us to find it contained a whole range of structural challenges, including significant problems with the roof. This resulted in a surveyor's valuation of £500K – miles away from our original offer price, and far from the asking price of £650K.

To put order into disorder, Lucy carefully listed the challenges highlighted in the report on to a spreadsheet and we both tried to put a price on each one, which we factored into a business plan. This included the cost of re-decoration and re-modelling designed to help us re-position the business from a pub nearer to a destination inn, and it also reflected the modest increases in sales and profits such a re-positioned product could bring. The result was a revised offer of £550K. This was not well received by the agent or vendor and after avoiding our calls for a number of days, we were eventually informed someone else had put in a better offer. Our hearts sank.

Lucy believed we could put in a slightly improved offer as the sales potential was possibly better than we predicted. However, we both agreed we weren't in a position to give up our well-paid jobs and risk being in a trap where we could not sell the business if we needed to because it was worth less than we paid for it. That situation could leave us trapped in debt.

So we agreed to walk away, £1,800 poorer thanks to the survey and having done a lot of hard work. But we were helped here by the discipline of Lucy's sales training. When pursuing sales contracts, she always had a strategy of 'wish', 'like' and 'walk' before entering negotiations. It's a sound strategy but in this case, because of the gulf between our revised offer and the asking price, we did not have the luxury of a wish-price or a like-price.

This left us with no other choice but to walk.

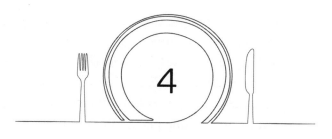

# 4

## The Little People

My first introduction to Lucy's parents, Tony and Eunice, was at Clematis Cottage when they came to check out the 'new boyfriend'. Before so much as a hello from Mum, she eyed me up and down and piped up: 'He's not *very* short'. Obviously, Lucy had compared me to a former, taller flame.

Anyway, who were they to talk? Neither of them was much over five feet, but what they lacked in height they certainly made up for in presence. Other sons-in-law are known to have christened them The Borrowers

Real northern folk, born-and-bred Lancastrians, they had an opinion on everything and on this day their opinion of me was forming fast. Fortunately, the cottage did a lot of the talking on my behalf – indeed, I found it difficult to get a word in. They immediately loved our home and took great pleasure in teasing me that I had hung a trellis upside down outside, growing a clematis into a point

I took to them as quickly as they took to the cottage. A few weeks later, Lucy went away with her sister for a few days and, without an invite, up popped Mum and Dad. Tony helped me to put up some pleached hornbeam trees and Eunice painted a watercolour of the garden. They ended up having supper and staying overnight. I suspected they were secretly checking that I was not up to mischief while their daughter was away;

but it felt like they had adopted me and possibly the cottage, falling for me and my home, hook, line and sinker.

Tony did a lot for Lucy and me at Clematis. There was one memorable piece of furniture that he made, an oak back door, which we still have today; we could not leave it in the sale and after four different storage locations, it takes pride of place at its final resting place, our current home.

Tony was a cabinet-maker by trade, one of the last few that came out of the world-famous cabinet-making company of Waring & Gillow, based in Lancaster. At the age of fourteen, he started a seven-year apprenticeship, documented on a piece of vellum that was then torn in two. The other half was not given back until the seven years were successfully completed. Tony then went on to become a journeyman, going all round the country fitting the furniture that had been made at the factory. He fitted out cruise ships, the Houses of Parliament, Buckingham Palace and many stately homes. Sadly, demand for this quality of craftsmanship declined greatly in the late 60s and, as mass production took over, the company closed in 1964 after 400 years of family ownership.

Tony and Eunice had both been married before. Derek, Eunice's first husband, tragically died when Lucy was a toddler and Eunice found it impossible to find anyone to match him until Tony turned up who was, as she describes it, 'knitted for me'.

Their life took a sudden turn when they upped sticks, sold everything and moved to France for more than ten years. They were inspired by a beautiful bed and breakfast they had stayed in at Harrogate and they wanted to escape on an adventure so they purchased a tumbledown farmhouse in Brantome, in the Dordogne region. Over two years Tony and Eunice created a five-bedroomed Chambre D'Hotes and a Gite – traditional French accommodation with a sitting room, two bedrooms and kitchenette – out of a rundown farmhouse and barns

Tony must have been at a similar age to me, early 50s, when he started out on their adventure and I am sure he really loved, endured and thrived on the relentless challenge to build and then operate a small business in a foreign country. No mean feat.

Their experience, help and support would prove invaluable when Lucy and I did finally manage to get our dream project up and running. But that was for another day. In the meantime, there was a wedding to consider.

# 5

# Marriages and Mortgages

Lucy and I were married in the chapel next door to our lovely Clematis Cottage. The disappointment of failing to secure the Sun Inn was put behind us as we directed our energies to making the day the most enjoyable and memorable it could be.

Now, in my experience of weddings there are two types – a bought one and a made one. Ours was most definitely one of the made varieties. We had a marquee erected in the garden, which was just starting to come into its own after three years' work, and Lucy made all the invitation cards.

On the day itself, Lucy's dad walked her down the aisle and my dad, by now a retired vicar, gave a lovely reading. My daughter Gemma dazzled us with a beautiful song, 'A Quiet Thing' and Lucy and I cemented our relationship with a poem by Robbie Burns, which we read to each other as part of the wedding service.

At the reception, the chef from the hotel I ran cooked lobster bisque and whole fillets of beef over a charcoal fire next to the marquee. My cousin Beth made the wedding cake, salads and lots of special extras; we had a chocolate fountain; and John and Jules came with their cheesecake. The whole event was overseen by an experienced banqueting manager, John Pitt, a hotel colleague of mine. And all was enjoyed by fifty-five friends and relatives on a most lovely sunny day.

It was as colourful as it was eventful. The bride was kept waiting by guests enjoying pre-wedding drinks in the bar; Lucy's niece Holly completed her public debut on the saxophone, which she would only do from the next room so no one could see her; my sister Sarah tripped onto her bad knee to great alarm; John, the head waiter for the day, in his exuberance somehow lost his footing and threw a cold and wet bottle of wine over a table, and the finale: my mother-in- law Eunice fell in the pond.

A very special day of fun, laughter, tears and utter joy.

We honeymooned in Croatia, and on our return quickly got back to the normal routine of life. That is, until 27<sup>th</sup> June when a letter arrived that was to turn our newly-married lives upside down. It came from the agent selling the Sun Inn telling us that an impending sale of the business had fallen through, and were we still interested in making a revised offer? It was, perhaps, fate; I had always secretly hoped this may happen, though I never dared express this out loud – not even to Lucy.

Things quickly became serious and intense. Returning to the diving meta-phor, we were preparing to climb the steps to the top board and execute a manoeuvre that would certainly take us out of our comfort zone and require complete belief in our own ability.

The purchase of the Sun Inn would have many twists and turns, but we were determined to take the plunge head-first and make a success of it. Of this we had no doubt.

We immediately organised a second viewing and when we got there spent the morning going through the Sun Inn's bookings diary and plotting the past overnight stays on to a spreadsheet to get a handle of midweek and weekend occupancy and establish past demand for rooms by time of year. Taking discounted rates into account, we saw the revenue listed for room sales on the diary was far greater than that recorded on the financial statements we had been given in the past. It seemed clear to us that while the vendor had tight control over liquor stocks and wages, there was little control over the rooms side of the business.

However, with this potential for further profit identified, we felt even more confident and went back with a slightly revised offer of £560K which the vendor considered. But it was not until almost three months later in September that the offer was accepted on the firm understanding we would complete within eight weeks. Our strategy of walking away had paid off. The property by this time had been on the market for seventeen months and the strategy of 'Marking Time' flashed in my mind – it had been a good call.

Our offer of £560K was £90K less than the original asking price – a fourteen per cent reduction. However, it was still £60K over the independent valuation. Our plan was to invest £90K to sort out the Sun Inn's structural problems and re-position the offer from a pub towards a destination inn. This would be achieved through redecoration, basic new furniture and fittings, a complete new set of standards together with a fresh, clean, open and honest approach.

But it would take a lot more cash than this and a great deal of effort to truly create our vision. This at least would stabilise the business and generate enough profit to justify the total investment of £650K from which we could build. So £560K was the right price for us.

The other financial factor we had to absorb was the additional costs and fees associated with purchasing the inn. These came to around £45K, which included solicitors, accountants, land registry, loan arrangement fees, stamp duty, stock and surveyors. It meant we were in for the long haul because the cost of getting in and the cost of getting out would have to be absorbed by profits over the years.

It was a frenetic time. We had to sell Clematis Cottage in eight weeks, secure a £320K loan from a bank as well as organise solicitors, accountants and prepare ourselves to launch a new business!

We got three estate agents round to value the cottage and pitch for the business of selling it. We tidied up all the paintwork, finished all the odd jobs and stage-managed the show rounds with log fires burning, coffee on the go and all clutter removed, and within the next ten days we had it on the market for £315K. Next was to secure the loan. I had prepared for this when we had put in our first offer for the inn and went with NatWest where I had banked for the last twenty years. Initially, all went well with the local branch, but when it came to reality it had to be passed to a regional office in Bristol. There it all got very sticky and was not going well, with one delay after another. The clock was ticking and we had not sold our house or raised money from the bank.

All we had was belief and absolute commitment.

As part of running the hotel in Daresbury, I was required to put myself out there in the local business community, and it so happened that I had been asked to host a meeting at the hotel and give a talk to the local chamber of commerce on my subject area. The brief was to keep it related to business and to be thought-provoking, so I gave a thirty-minute talk on return on capital investment, having so recently been inspired by my company's chief executive on the subject.

The talk went OK, and as you do on these occasions you pass business cards around and network. A card that shone out to me was the one with HSBC bank all over it. Those words 'strike while the iron's hot' rang in my ears and I immediately manoeuvred my way over to the bank official to request a quiet word. I then proceeded to explain that I wanted to borrow £320K for a business. Cheeky, I know, but we desperately needed the loan. That was at 7.30pm in the evening; by 9.30am next morning, I had a call from an executive at HSBC who wanted to make an appointment to see me, so I guess the talk the previous night wasn't a complete disaster.

By the end of the week we'd met and our application was processed. The following Tuesday, I had a call to say could I meet a regional executive from HSBC at 11am at the Daresbury hotel. This was awkward because the meeting was to be held at my workplace and in work time. However, I said yes, and hurriedly orchestrated a quiet corner in the lounge. He arrived at 11am with the same colleague I had met earlier and with whom I had already completed the application with business plan, etc. The regional executive asked me just one question: 'Why do you want to run your own business?' I told him it was to get out of a corporate environment and be in control of my own destiny. Then I shut up and allowed a short, slightly awkward silence.

The interest rate would be two per cent above base, he said. I allowed another further short silence and then replied that I was looking for 1.5 per cent above base. He asked what I'd based that figure on, so I mentioned the ongoing negotiations I was having with NatWest. I said I was keen to move more quickly than they were going but that they had offered 1.5 per cent above base or, more truthfully, that's what I was asking them for.

Finally, the HSBC executive and I shook on 1.75 per cent above base, and within twenty minutes the deal was done. I never saw him again; it was all handled from there on in by a nice HSBC business advisor called Helen. She was very supportive and visited us at the Inn on many occasions over the first three years. But make no mistake, the bank held first rights on the property and could call in the loan whenever they wanted. And to help assess the strength of the business, they would keep a close eye on our quarterly profit and loss accounts. This was my biggest personal financial deal to date and it felt both scary and exhilarating and I could not wait to get home and tell Lucy we'd secured the mortgage.

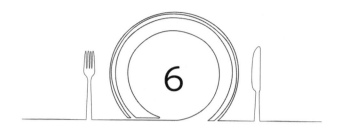

# 6

# Leaving all that was secure

Clematis Cottage was the first house I could afford following my divorce and it held a special place in my heart. The way I remodelled and dressed the cottage reflected my personality, style and the direction I wanted my life to lead. It was both a painful period in my life as well as a very joyous one; I really loved that cottage. At dinner parties, Lucy tells people it was the cottage that won her over and that the love for Mark came later – but the truth is, they were the same thing.

So you can imagine the wrench after living there for more than seven years and finding happiness to see it sold, and all the money and safety the cottage had brought exchanged for the insecurity of a new business.

Because we decided to put the cottage on the market for a realistic price, bang in the middle of the three estimates and not discounted, we had an offer within three weeks of going on the market and the sale was completed within seven weeks at the end of November 2005.

The day we moved out and handed over the keys, I broke down in tears and was inconsolable. I believed I was doing the right thing, but it was like losing a dear friend who'd helped me to discover myself truly for the first time in my life. Now it was gone and I would have to go out on my own. Of course, I had Lucy and was not going it alone; but the person I wanted to be and the life I wanted to lead, had been expressed in that dear cottage.

Now the cottage and I were linked no more.

Amazingly, our funds were all in place within the eight-week ultimatum from the Sun Inn's vendors. It just goes to show how a fixed date can focus the mind. It certainly did ours.

Lucy did not have a house to sell, but over the previous couple of years had helped me in investing money into Clematis Cottage to develop the property further with landscaping, garage and new windows. She, like me, put everything she had into buying this business; in terms of our initial capital, I put in about eighty per cent and she put in the rest, and we were jointly responsible for the business mortgage. We agreed that it was going to take every single ounce of effort from both of us to make this a success and from here on any profit that we made was going to be split fifty-fifty irrespective of the capital invested, and when eventually selling the business this original capital would be returned and any capital gained would be split again fifty-fifty.

But before we could take over the Sun Inn we would effectively be homeless. Our furniture had to go into storage and we sofa-hopped at our respective parents' homes for the next six weeks. Then we moved into Lucy's sister's house that just happened to be vacant while the agent, solicitors and vendors dragged their feet. The vendors had demanded completion within eight weeks and we were now into three months of having sold our home and desperately hoping that our employers would not get wind of our business plans just in case it all fell through. We were definitely in the risk phase and it felt like a prison break, hoping they were not going to discover the tunnel we had dug out for ourselves.

At such times, family and friends are everything, and Lucy and I were thankfully very lucky to have the most magnificent support, in abundance.

An early port of call was to Lucy's cousin's legal practice, Alan Garrick of Lancaster. Alan was extremely generous with his time and patience. He has a cautious, enthusiastic approach and he provided us with great advice and contacts locally, including accountants, surveyors and so on. As family, he also charged for the work at less than the going rate, not that we had any idea what that was. Alan and his wife June were in private practice, and with their exemplary attitude and approach, personified what it was like to run your own business. As cautious as Alan was, he was not afraid to take calculated risks, both with us as novices in setting up our own business and also with the Sun Inn's vendors, who were proving very difficult when it came to providing information we needed to get us over the all-important contract exchange 'touchline'.

Christmas came and went and it was not till towards the end of January that we eventually exchanged contracts on the sale. It was a tricky manoeuvre as we had to give three months' notice to our employers, and yet the vendor now wanted to complete within four weeks of exchange. Eventually we agreed on eight weeks and contracts were exchanged. But it was Alan who made this all happen.

On handing in our notices, word spread quickly that we were buying our own business; everybody in the organisation knew about it immediately and we received some interesting responses.

My immediate boss, who I found tricky to handle, was in fact broadly supportive of our venture, but mildly surprised that we were taking such a bold move. Fortunately, he allowed me to use a three-weeks' holiday allowance, and let me off one week of notice. Others seemed to see our venture as extremely risky, though many were privately envious of our escaping the corporate environment. Those were the sort who, when push came to shove, would back down from taking a dive into the entrepreneurial pool. However, I do think one or two were genuinely inspired by our move and went on to start their own enterprises.

So, there we were: we had resigned our jobs, sold our house and signed on the dotted line to purchase. All that was left now was eight weeks of intense and exciting preparation. Game on!

True to form, Eunice and Tony shot up to Kirkby Lonsdale like a couple of hares once they knew we were visiting what was then called the Sun Hotel to check out further important details. Without our knowledge or an invite, in walked Mum and Dad as we were looking over the information the vendors had left for us. They couldn't help themselves; they just loved a new project, a new life, a new adventure, and no six hour round trip was going to stop them. After another tour of the pub they kept muttering things like, 'Do you know what you are taking on?' and, 'I do hope you know what you are taking on.'

Yes, we knew. However, unlike they, who had done it on their own, we didn't know just how stretching and challenging our project would prove to be and what an enormous supporting part they would play.

Once back in Birmingham, we explained our plans and how we were going to strip the bedrooms of everything so we could decorate and re-fit. To which Tony said, 'What do you want? tables? furniture? Tell me what you want and I'll make it for you.'

So a week later I dropped off a rough sketch with dimensions of a bedhead and side tables to go with it and two weeks later there it was – the most beautiful oak furniture with spade legs in the Adam style, so appropriate for our little place. It was not just his skill in making the furniture, but his choice of the right design.

That weekend, Lucy and I went out and bought bedside lamps and cushions to do a full sample bedroom; but we realised a desk was needed to complement the bedhead and so the request went in to Tony. By the day we left to make our own way up to Kirkby Lonsdale and take possession of the property, he had made five sets of furniture, including the desks and a mobile buffet unit with marble top for the restaurant – within weeks, and out of a tiny shed at the bottom of a suburban garden.

Between exchange and completion of our purchase, we organised ourselves the best we could, creating a new bookings diary, arranging for two large posters to cover up both entrances while we were redecorating to show locals our plans and what we hoped to deliver. We also had to finalise the appointment of a new chef, write the staff handbook, order carpets, beds, bedhead fabric, soft furnishings, and pack up for our imminent move – all while working full-time.

On the day of the move, we loaded the new furniture very carefully into the hired van. Pulling away with the vehicle full of all our equipment and furniture felt just wonderful. A new life had begun.

We travelled up to Lancaster on the Sunday, staying at another of Lucy's sisters, to be close and ready for the handover first thing Monday morning, on the way picking up my daughter Gemma who was able to help us for the first week, and then come back after a week to help for a further two. Gemma was in her early twenties and desperately trying to make her way in musical theatre. She, too, was a great support and would quickly get stuck in with the ten-hour working-day regime ripping out carpets, stripping walls and so on. I felt it was good that she could see her Dad and Lucy making their own way in life and how tough it was at the beginning. I'm sure the work ethic was already in her and hoped this experience would confirm just how tough life could be. Gemma clearly had talent but I believe the values of hard work and the will to succeed she subsequently witnessed may, in a small way, have helped inspire her own subsequent success in the West End musical theatre business over the next eleven years of our ownership of the Sun Inn. In any case we were very grateful for the help she gave before she went on to work on shows in London's West End.

The vendor's area manager and relief pub manager were the only staff present on the day of the handover. There had been seven or eight staff on the books when we came to exchange, but by now they had dwindled to three part-time staff. The kitchen had been closed for two weeks, so there was no need to count the food stock, although the fridges and freezers still had food in them. The liquor stock had also been run down and the stock-taker quickly produced a closing stock cash figure. We then moved on to the inventory of furniture and fittings, not that we wanted to keep anything, and considered it of little importance to begin with.

As we progressed, I realised they were having difficulty in tracking down all the items and I smelled cash! As a consequence, I started to vigorously pursue each item line by line and had them chasing all over the building looking for TVs, fridges, pictures, ornaments and such, or agreeing they were missing. After an hour, by this time 11.30am or so, in rolled Tony and Eunice.

Tony was his usual forthright self: 'Christ! Have you not started to get working yet; what are you doing? The van is not even unloaded.'

Lucy hastily pulled them away for coffee. The cat-and-mouse game over missing items on the inventory went on for another forty-five minutes, after which time the vendor's representative gave in. We agreed a rebate of £500 for goods not present that we never really wanted anyway. They hurriedly gave us the rundown on the keys, gas, electricity, and water cut-off point and that was it. We received the call from our solicitor to confirm completion and the vendors' representatives sped away. The building was ours.

# The First 21 Days

When you give up your well-paid job and home, you become very aware just how vulnerable you are, and without any income for the ensuing twenty-one days – the time we had given ourselves to transform and re-open the inn – that £500 came in very handy. It would at least pay to keep the family workforce fed and watered!

Those twenty-one days did not feel like work; the experience was more like a cross between a working holiday and a sabbatical from my corporate working life with the constant anxiety of no return. This was it, no going back to regular salary, we had to make it work and every day that went by was one step nearer to our new refreshed product and the prospect of making our own profit. The goal of a new refreshed product seemed elusive, for every two steps forward we would go back one, with some sort of challenge; on some days we would go back two steps and only move forward one. It was on those sorts of days that I was so conscious of holding my nerve, so very strong in the belief that Lucy and I would find a way to overcome every challenge and make this work.

The power of belief is incredible; it's got people to the moon and made people carry out the most extraordinary feats. Belief needs to be nurtured, encouraged, supported. Looking back, I realise the important roles Tony, Eunice, Terry and Aileen played.

We now had just twenty and a half days left to turn the place around; but before we started there was one short, but vitally important, task to perform before we closed and that was to sell a few drinks over the counter to officially launch our trading year 2005-6.

This was done on the advice of our new accountants, Moore and Smalley. They advised us to set up a partnership rather than a limited company and that if we made a loss in the first two or three years of trading we would be able to claim against tax paid in previous years. With the amount we were going to spend in the next twenty-one days, it was clear we were going to make a significant loss in this tax year against a very small amount of sales made on that day.

Next we unpacked the van and put up the two large posters on the inn doors, whited out the windows and, following a group tour of the building, we each found a least-bad room for us to check into.

Fortunately, the laundry company used by the old owners turned up early afternoon to take away the linen and were kind enough to leave a few sheets and towels. Meanwhile, the girls washed blankets in the laundry room and were able to dry them before the evening using the tumble-dryer. Grim as the building was, at least we had clean sheets to sleep in.

During the afternoon, I filled the first of what would eventually be ten full transit-van loads of rubbish ready to take to the tip the following morning. Then I had a quick trip to the shops before they shut, to feed the troops. Venturing into the kitchen, I tried to turn on the extraction fans only to find they did not work. A commercial kitchen without extract and intake of air is a non-starter, and after the engineer's visit, it was confirmed that a new fan was required at £600 (not budgeted for). We endeavoured to claim this back from the vendor, but they were having none of it and said it was working when they left. Could this be part of the reason the kitchen had been out of action for the last two weeks? Perhaps I should have smelled a rat when I first realised they had closed the kitchen.

As the hours and days ticked by and more and more rubbish was stripped out, the job appeared to grow exponentially.

Plans were in place to get a little head of steam up as I'd organised to have the manager's flat, consisting of four rooms and a bathroom, to be cleared out and decorated a week before completion; but the decorators were a week behind. Anyway, at least in seven days we could have this area carpeted and have somewhere clean for us to sleep.

It was 5.30pm on the seventh day when the carpet fitters completed the final room of the flat. They'd made good the floorboards as they were in a bit of a state but the fitters were unaware they'd banged a nail right through a water pipe. Just as they sped away, Tony and Eunice went to their bedroom below the flat to find water pouring through the ceiling and all over their bed. It was but one of a host of challenges we experienced throughout those frantic twenty-one days.

So where was the turn-off valve for the water? I'd been shown briefly at the handover and went immediately to the shut-off tap but it didn't stop the water pouring into the room. A few weeks later it transpired that there were two mains water pipes into the building and at some point they joined up, a most unusual situation brought about by generations of renovations and amalgamation of separate buildings to create the inn we now had. Without being able to obtain a plumber, up came the newly laid carpet, the source of the problem was identified and Tony did his magic, inserting a new piece of copper pipe. How he did it without turning off the water is still a mystery, but he did – as he did when he handled so many other crises that arose with the building, accompanied by the customary expletives and followed by a fag after each job.

By the end of the first week everything had been stripped out and got rid of and we were left with fourteen days to decorate, fit out and re-model our Inn. Lucy had been away for a few days of the first week as she still had work commitments but she was now back in the fold and trying to put order into disorder at a hectic pace. Each day out came a list of jobs for the crew and each would fight to get them achieved, constantly looking for tools and equipment that someone else had borrowed. We could not really afford a team of decorators so it was a do-it-yourself job. We were a little naughty getting the flat done, but without this it would have been chaos as on the Monday of the second week the furniture from our cottage arrived from storage.

It took most of the day to put the furniture in place and sort out the flat and place the rest of the furniture around the building. The following day the new beds arrived, which took almost all the morning to sort out and store, and from then on there were constant interruptions either from suppliers to set up accounts, or things we needed to order and collect; enquiries to be handled; training to be received on tills; accounting systems, credit cards, and so on —all in all, it felt as though everyone was after our time, leaving us with none to get on with the job in hand. To add to the mix, the new head chef that we'd recruited arrived and, although briefed and initially happy to clean and redecorate the kitchen so that, for his benefit, we could take him on a week earlier, now made it clear that the task did not enthral him.

Other warning signs emerged with complaints about how far away he had to park his car each day and how we would have to secure a parking permit for him (which we did asap) and then what he could and couldn't cook because of the state of the kitchen, which he had visited before taking on the job. It was a fiery cocktail, and no matter how early we started and how late we finished we could just not get to everything. Of course, the more tired we became the less efficient and more niggly we all were. How we got through the next twelve days is all a bit of a blur as each day and evening went into the next. There was one famous day when Lucy and I were being trained on the tills, I closed my eyes and briefly fell asleep standing up. There were two occasions that I do remember clearly. Firstly, a ten-hour trip to IKEA to bring back wardrobes, mirrors and attachments all in our small Mini. Lucy was barricaded in the car and boxes were sticking out of the back. We looked a right sight. Fortunately, we didn't arrive back until after midnight so nobody saw what a farce this was. Secondly, the first night we spent in the newly decorated flat was on the floor, although on a clean carpet. There was a full moon, no curtains and the charm of the ring-a-ding-ding of the church bells and the owls hooting in the churchyard. We squeezed each other tightly and neither could believe how lovely it was to have escaped from the corporate world. None of this felt like work; tired as we were, we just felt so very happy.

We may not have had the corporate support of a big company we were used to, but you could be sure Eunice and Tony would fill the vacuum. They'd followed us to the Sun Inn with bags packed for three weeks, as well as two cats, plenty of cigarettes and Tony full of expletives yet to be uttered and grief yet to be given. They came with utter devotion to the cause and the love for us to succeed.

Mum's job was the toilets. She washed down and sanded all the paint-work, stripped the floor on her hands and knees revealing not only the true colours of the tiles but also revealing her grit and determination. She painted the area out in Farrow and Ball sugar-bag light and cream. The toilets really needed gutting, but with limited time and money she made them look fresh and presentable and a hundred per cent better than they were.

Dad built a new back-fitting to the bar, installed shelving and sorted out plumbing for the cappuccino machine, in between sorting out one build-ing challenge after another with the frequent cry: 'Bloody hell, is anything square in this bloody place!'

In their seventies, Tony and Eunice worked ten hours every day and after a good supper, cooked by yours truly, they were tucked up in bed by 9pm and ready to start at 8am the next morning. The northern temperament is sometimes *blunt* and after ten days of relentless work and much frustration with us, the building and the amount of work yet to do, Tony gave it to me like a bullet to the forehead.

'You're taking too much on, Mark,' he said. 'You'll never get this finished to open in eleven days. Best to forget about the bedrooms; just concen-trate on getting the downstairs finished and open. Bloody ridiculous!' With that, he stormed off to bed with smoke coming out of his ears as well as his mouth, and with a final charge, 'And if you think your friends from California will help, you can think again: there's too much to do!'

We were in crisis; not just because we were behind, but because we feared we were about to lose Tony and Eunice's help, which we desperately needed. Nor did I want to be the reason for a family fall-out.

That night, with a heavy head, I couldn't sleep. Within the hour was I dressed and ready to paint through the night; I managed to get the ceiling and walls of the bar completed by the morning. Tony and I barely spoke during the morning and Lucy and Mum lay low while we cracked on with tasks in silence until I departed for the station to pick up my old diving coach, mentor and lifelong friend Terry and his wife Aileen, who had come over from California specifically to help us.

With barely time for any pleasantries, they were in there working on the bedrooms, stripping wallpaper and sanding down. It was like the cavalry arriving and they, like Tony and Eunice, were no spring chickens. Terry was in his late sixties and not afraid of hard work or getting his hands dirty; although Aileen, a little younger and more agile, was the powerhouse to compensate. Most importantly, there was instant mutual respect between the couples. They also possessed wisdom and knew the task was pretty impossible; yet neither couple was going to let Lucy or me down. The impossible task had not gone away, but the raging fire between Tony and I had died down and we could both now see a glimmer of hope. After forty-eight sleepless hours, I could now kip with a little more ease.

We had asked too much of Eunice and Tony and nearly brought them to breaking point. How grateful we are to them. They continued to support us in so many ways over the eleven years of ownership, Tony doing the most wonderful cabinet-work and shop-fitting: making tables and bar tops; making and fitting numerous doors, locks and handles; and Mum ironing and folding napkins, washing up and caring for us all throughout.

As much as this business was our business, it was theirs too and it made them and us feel very proud. We were living their dream of the past and they were living ours.

Our plan had been to strip out all the rubbish, clean, decorate and re-model the inn with new carpets, beds, Tony's new oak bedroom furniture and the furniture we had from Clematis Cottage to create a fresh new look. By 2pm on the day before the launch party with the Kirkby locals, we'd completed four bedrooms, bar, cellar, kitchen and toilets and were just left with the restaurant to finish. This we all quickly cleaned, part-painted and dressed with our furniture from home. By 7pm, we were waxing the floors, much to the annoyance of one or two loyal family members who wanted to know why I couldn't just stop adding finishing touches.

Finally, the job was done. We'd made it.

# 8

# Opening for Business

The following morning, we took down the posters on the front door, cleared the smeared windows and prepared for a reception with the locals. John and Jules from Churchmouse Cheese had helped with this by distributing invites on our behalf. We received the most wonderful welcome from all who came, with many bouquets of flowers and masses of cards wishing us good luck. Our very dear Mum and Dad presented us with a pub bell to call time and Lucy and I made brief speeches. It was all a great success, except for rumbles from the chef who was not happy over the timings of the canapés; he left the reception in a huff.

We opened fully to the public on the Tuesday. We'd cut it fine and only just said goodbye to Terry and Aileen, whose valuable help had ensured the bedrooms were on stream in time for the first guests. They'd also supplied much of the goodwill and humour that oiled the wheels, helping everyone to complete what seemed an almost impossible, but nonetheless impressive, makeover against the clock. This, like our wedding, felt like a made inn rather than a bought one; and a great deal richer for it both in cash terms and the feel the place exuded.

Now we had to get trading. This was to be a baptism of fire as Lucy and I quickly got to grips with pulling pints, serving food and introducing systems and processes. From day one, the business took off and the place was regularly full for lunch and dinner.

We'd purposely limited the number of tables in the bar and restaurant so we could cope, but the poor chef could not. We instantly arranged for an agency chef the next day to help him, but even with this support his mood and behaviour got worse and by the Friday morning he handed in his notice. Was it our fault, or was it his? There was no time for an inquest; he gave us a week's notice and by the next day the agency had provided a temp head chef and another second chef. We wasted no time and parted company with our unhappy chef the very next day. I think he was as shocked as we were that he was going so quickly. This was eleven years ago. Chefs are in much greater demand today, but the episode quickly taught us how important your suppliers are. Without this help from the local agency, we would have been in real trouble; especially as the coming weekend was Easter Bank Holiday. It is traditional then for the caravan and camping parks to open up for the season, and visitor numbers swell. Lucy looked after the bar with one part-time member of staff and I covered the restaurant with my daughter, who returned for the opening, and one other part-time member of staff for both lunch and dinner. And, bless them, Mum and Dad stayed on for the whole weekend to wash up. At around 10pm on our first Saturday, Lucy and I both took five minutes out after working from 7am, starting with me cooking breakfast before the chefs arrived, and Lucy serving, to 10 pm solid.

We walked outside the inn and looked through the windows to a packed house and Lucy said: 'What the hell have we done buying a pub?' High on adrenalin and bowled over with success we giggled and hugged, shaking from nervous energy. We had many challenges to face but tonight we were on a winner.

The locals and the first few residents got the vision. It was not just a name change from the Sun Hotel (clearly it hadn't been a hotel but a pub), it was now an inn – so much more than a pub. The hospitality levels and atmosphere we created from a friendly home-from-home approach, where guests were treated as if they were invited into your own home, was argu-ably unique for Kirkby Lonsdale. Standards such as the finest pillow-top mattresses for the beds and the crystal glasses we served wine in took it to another level.

The product, however, was still very much incomplete, like a sketch yet to be painted in oil. Integral to the product were the locals, since they were as friendly as we were and so it was essential we got it right for them. In turn, they created the atmosphere for the residents who travelled from afar and would tell the world.

These first few days of tough trading with long hours taught us such a lot. Firstly, the business potential was so much bigger than we had anticipated. Secondly, Kirkby Lonsdale was wealthy not only in money but also in kindness and friendship. We needed to get tooled up for a much bigger business before our stamina ran out as bookings were flying in. More urgently we needed to get all the takings we received since opening to the bank and work out how we were going to account for it in our books. The flat, with a desk stuffed full of cash, had the smell and look of an Italian mafia den about it. Most definitely the business was up and running.

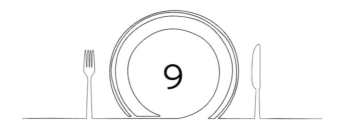

# Return on Capital Investment
# (the overview)

You will recall that I believed return on capital investment was an area of the business that I, as a manager, felt I should have been exposed to much earlier on in my career. After truly understanding demand and market opportunity, it is, I believe, one of the fundamental principles a manager should know and thoroughly understand if a hospitality business is to grow profitably.

It is, however, one of those areas that managers are often not exposed to or shy away from due to the complicated indices, fancy jargon and varying methods, leaving it to the world of hotel and pub investors, accountants, consultants and valuers. This is a great mistake so don't be put off. At the end of the book I have designed a chapter, Return On Capital Investment (the detail simplified), so that anyone reading this and wanting to take the leap of faith to either buy or invest in a hospitality business can quickly master and understand this most important area and get to grips with assessing both the current value, and the potential value of a business with further financial investment. As this chapter may require studying rather than reading for general interest, I have put the detail at the end of the book. It was without question this understanding and insight that bought Lucy and me our financial success, which we were very fortunate to have gained and mastered towards the end of our corporate lives before purchasing the Sun Inn.

There are a number of people who believe the hospitality business is easy. Maybe they think of retiring early to run a life-style business or they see the front of the business from the customer's side and like the idea of owning it. The reality is quite different and often the venture fails. This is especially the case in tenancies. I have often observed new owners who come with a lot of enthusiasm, and after the shock of hard work and long hours they manage to get to grips with the operation, but fail to understand all the pertinent aspects about return on capital investment, and they leave within three years, often financially worse off than when they started. As a general manager running a large corporate hotel, I've experienced taking over from a manager who implemented a multi-million-pound refurbishment. Yet the profits were no more than they were before the refurbishment started. This was because there wasn't the correct balance of capital expenditure in revenue and profit-generating areas compared to infrastructure. Asking a company to spend further money to rectify the problem of an over-invested hotel was a tall order to say the least.

A corporate boss said to me one time 'you can only spend capital once'. An obvious statement, but what he was really saying was that you only have one chance to spend capital so spend it wisely. Should you make a poor investment, you could lose a lot of money or, worse still, bankrupt the business. It can take a long time to amass enough money to start up on your own. I paid a mortgage on my house for more than twenty years before I could sell my house and use the capital to buy the business. So the subject of return on capital investment is serious and one that is essential for you to master if you go it alone. On the brighter side, once you have mastered it, you will be able to make your own clear assessment as to the value of a business, not just as it stands today, but what its value may be in the future with wise and prudent investment. That is exactly what Lucy and I did.

With this understanding, we were able to make transformational returns on our various investment opportunities. By investing in one area of the business and making good returns in that area we were also able to bring a greater value to the overall business, a sort of double-return, if you like.

This return on investment was <u>not</u> done at the expense of either the staff or the customer, or by asset-stripping. Quite the reverse: by carefully planning capital investment, the customer can receive a far better product, which results in increased revenue. This business increase could require you to take on more staff and perhaps necessitate staff development/promotion, and as a consequence improve their remuneration. In our case this carefully planned investment also preserved an historic Grade II listed building for generations to come.

Without this financial map and compass or without understanding the financial models, it would have been like sailing in the middle of the ocean not knowing which direction to go in and running out of resources fast.

What I love about our industry is that you have to learn such a diverse range of skills. As well as being that Diplomat, Door Mat and Aristocrat that David referred to, you also have to be a financial wizard, an interiors guru, a health-and-hygiene specialist, a food critic, a barrister (if you have to represent yourself at a tribunal, as I did), a manager of people, a marketer and a shopkeeper. No wonder many of us hospitality entrepreneurs have a low boredom threshold as we skate across the myriad of disciplines that we are suppose to be expert in. I am reminded of a definition of an expert, ex is a 'has-been' and a spurt is just a little bit better than a dribble! There were times when we had to master new skills when we certainly felt like that kind of expert.

What I am trying to say is that you don't need to be an expert on the return of capital investment, you just have to master the principles and apply the insights gained if you want to confidently and exponentially grow the business.

Now turn to the final chapter Return on Capital Expenditure (the detail), if you want to study the map and compass for financial capital. Otherwise read on.

# BLDs

At the Sun Inn, the weekly rosters were staffed in three shifts covering breakfast, lunch and dinner. Lucy and I featured in them all seven days a week for the first twelve months; there was no escape. We referred to them affectionately as the BLDs, not breakfast, lunch, dinner but Bloody Long Days.

One enterprising former boss once told me: 'If you do not feel out of control you're not going fast enough.' But this first year was not a sprint, it was a marathon. We'd already completed a half-marathon in purchasing the Sun Inn and getting the doors open for business. This next marathon followed immediately and swiftly on its heels; and, yes, on many occasions Lucy and I felt out of control and let each other know it. Tiredness can be a form of mental torture and sometimes during this period we felt like prisoners of the building. We knew survival was dependent on not letting each other down but on one memorable occasion the torture got to us, and we broke.

It must have been six or seven weeks after opening, a Friday, the start of a busy weekend. By now, the normal routine was Lucy up from 7am preparing to cook breakfast, opening the post and doing the guest bills. I'd be cleaning the bar and restaurant before the guests came down. We'd crack on serving breakfast and, after washing up, go on to prepare for lunch.

Lucy would do the banking, post accounts or pay some bills. I'd then run lunch and Lucy would help with housekeeping and/or lunch until about 3pm when we would break for a couple of hours. Sometimes there was no proper break and we'd work through, perhaps organising the finishing of rooms that we hadn't managed to get back to letting during the three-week closure; or maybe we'd rush out to buy new doors or equipment to bring the building up to standard.

On this particular day, we were knackered. We'd been working through the break all week in order to get jobs done and we just needed to sleep for a couple of hours before the Friday-night rush. But our part-time member of staff phoned in sick for the 3pm shift – at 3pm! There was no one we could call. We started out by both being courageous, saying 'you go for a rest', 'no, you go for a rest'. But neither of us would back down and we both snapped. An argument developed. In temper, I closed the front door and turned out the lights. It was fortunate that no guests were in the building, but some were due to arrive and check in at any minute.

I said, 'If you don't rest now, there will be no business.' In a slight state of shock, Lucy went for a break; by 10pm we were talking again and she let me go to bed early at 10pm while she finished serving at the bar, locked up and slid into bed at midnight. There were a few occasions like this, but that one stuck in my mind.

Those days were brutal. We were often clocking up a 112-hour week, but as time went by we did start to build a team. We had now recruited a head chef John, a second chef Sarah and a kitchen commis called Sammy to complement our Czech kitchen porter Ondres. He'd walked in off the street the day after Mum and Dad had gone back to Walsall. We were so desperate, we employed him on the spot. He and his girlfriend, now wife, Suzannah worked with us for the next two years until they went back home to the Czech Republic. Ondres was brilliant. From two domestic sinks he would wash up and dry by hand all the pots and pans the kitchen threw at him; along with all plates, cutlery and china, for sometimes as many as 100 lunches and 50 dinners on a Saturday, always leaving the place clean and tidy. Just as he left to go back home, we built a brand-new kitchen with an automatic dishwasher. No person could have replaced Ondres, but fortunately our job was made much easier with the addition of a new dishwasher machine.

By the September, Tom had joined us. He wanted a gap year and work experience before looking for his 'career' job, and we gave him a one-year full-time floor supervisor role, allowing us to have one or two evenings off. The Sun Inn was our baby and it was difficult to relax, hearing it all go on while we were in the flat upstairs, and often disturbed by some challenge or another. If we went out for the evening we would dread returning just in case there had been any problems in our absence. Mostly it was OK, but occasionally not. We would always brace ourselves for the worse, returning with trepidation from what often was a much-needed escape.

To afford our increasing numbers of staff, we couldn't sit still, and in the midst of these BLDs we had somehow to fit in the first of our two major building projects, replacing the roof and developing the bedrooms.

Renewing the roof of a Grade 2 listed building of commercial premises next to sacred land belonging to the church is not straightforward. We first had to carry out a detailed survey of the roof space and obtain a specification of works, as well as satisfying the conservation officer of sound timbers and trusses in case of replacement, and also ensure the absence of protected bats. Next, was to set up a JCT contract to ensure work was done to a certain standard and was safe for commercial premises. My mate Phil, a chartered surveyor, kindly set up the contract and I filled in the blanks and then eventually we got out to tender, which took hours of administration and time that we did not have. Eventually we commissioned the works, but then on the first day, found that the contractor had omitted to get approval to put scaffolding on the churchyard lawn. Formal approval would take weeks. Fortunately, I had volunteered to cut the grass on the church lawn a couple of weeks earlier, not that I wasn't busy enough already, but it did provide the goodwill to enable the rector to fast-track approval. The roof was due to take three months; in the end it took six and delayed the much needed repainting on the outside of the building.

With all that going on, we had even less time to devote to developing the bedroom product. Ironically, funding was flying in. We'd built up a cash reserve of £24K by each doing the work of two people day-in day-out; our accountants' plan to reclaim tax from a loss the previous year resulted in at £20K tax rebate, and an endowment policy I'd taken out twenty-five years before matured, providing £21K. Never before in my life had I been so cash-rich and time-poor; nor had such an entrepreneurial thirst developed that could not be slaked.

As I explain in the chapter about return on investment, the best opportunity was always going to be in rooms; not only financially but also physically in terms of using otherwise wasted space. We couldn't wait to exploit the demand for rooms that was emerging. The building was in the shape of a hollow square, although from the outside it looks L-shaped. You can see from old drawings of the fire certificate with the old numbering system, that the office and the laundry were perfect to develop. The laundry had already been contracted out and we found another store we could install a small domestic washing machine. We also cleared the largest room at the front of the inn which had been used by the previous owners as an office and liquor storeroom. This was to be the best room in the house and, by splitting the laundry in two, we could create a bathroom for it and for the second largest bedroom next door. Meanwhile, room 8 was a small single room and bedroom 10 a double, both without en-suite facilities – prime candidates for combining to make one excellent double room with private bathroom.

We knew we had enough demand to fill a new room and we knew we could charge more for rooms with a bathroom. What we didn't know was whether or not our customers would pay for higher, de-luxe accommodation. Going to that higher level was particularly important as a true destination inn needed a high-grade product, and so this was our opportunity to test the market with three rooms before converting all the others.

With very little time on our hands, we contracted an interior designer and project manager. Charles Batchelor provided all the technical and administrative support and quickly got on to the task, liaising with the conservation officer, planning and building control and contractors, and by our first Christmas all the plans were in place to close for three weeks in January to complete the works. We would take a much-needed two-week holiday, Mum and Dad (and cat) would move in and all would be well. By all accounts they endured a horrendous ordeal, often being left by the builders with no electricity, water or heating. Tony, all too familiar with building sites and renovations, was in his element. He could see it was not a smooth ride. The main contractor was a firm called Derek De'ath and you can imagine what the locals and Tony had to say about Mr Death, can't you? We complicated the build by having to have both a new hot-water boiler and a new and bigger supply of cold water to feed the new bathrooms, as if the current two water supplies were not enough! We got back from our holiday in the nick of time, adjusting bathroom layouts and cleaning up the mess and bringing the project in on time to open for our new bookings.

The deluxe rooms sold at a thirty to forty per cent premium to our other rooms and were the first to be booked up. It seemed the more we invested in this lovely building, the more it responded with charming our customers and handsomely returning the investment.

Those of you who've embarked on a fitness regime or performed sport to a high level will no doubt recall that the start is full of excitement, and then you begin to face really tough barriers. You become sluggish as your body adjusts and builds strength and then you come out the other end stronger, more confident and positive as your performance improves and the exercise becomes almost a drug that you cannot get off. Well, by this stage in April, the BLD training had put us through its paces and we'd come out the other end stronger and fitter and ready to move the business to another level. Our initiation was complete and we felt we'd passed the test. But there were still challenges that needed addressing if we were to achieve our goal of a five-star Inn.

# 11

# Divide and Conquer

Working morning, noon and night had served three important purposes. Firstly, we needed money to carry out work on the inn and we were in no position to borrow more; even if we had been, we didn't want to pay any more interest to the bank. Within the first nine months we were able to save an additional £24K as we were literally doing two people's jobs as well as our own. Secondly, we got to know our customers intimately – they were the only friends we had time to see. They gave us wonderful feedback, kindness and all sorts of tips and ideas. They told us what they liked and what they didn't like; not just the big things such as dated avocado bathroom suites with plastic taps, but little things like the music or the temperature of the beer or range of food items. Overarching all of this, what they wanted was us; not because Lucy and I were particularly special, but because they wanted hosts to relate to who made them feel recognised, welcomed and that they belonged. These locals were perhaps the most valuable ingredient of the whole product; they brought the inn alive, created the atmosphere and made the tourists and overnight visitors feel part of something special.

We also recognised that if we were going to get off this relentless treadmill and start to develop the business, we would have to recruit another Mark and Lucy; otherwise as we drew away from the floor, the business would be affected. Recruiting another 'us' came in the form of Steve and Janine around April the following year. We didn't recruit them as a pair, they just happened to join us the same week, and they had similar traits, loyalty and caring natures. Beyond that, they were worlds apart. Steve, just into his thirties, was outgoing, fun-loving, reactive, jumpy, not so organised. Janine in her early twenties, was modest, organised, cautious, process-driven and a planner.

We played them to their strengths. Their personalities rubbed off on us and ours on them. Often, we would be asked if Steve was my brother or son and Janine my daughter. Occasionally a guest would confuse me with Steve, a compliment for me, but not so good for Steve's ego. Of course, we always brushed it off, but deep down I would have been proud to have been their dad. They are lovely people, and we adopted them as family, as we did with so many wonderful members of staff who worked for us. It was satisfying to see them flourish.

Steve was the master of customer hostmanship, just brilliant with guests. An entrepreneurial stint at Bentham golf club doing everything himself meant he could do each task at breakneck speed, often starting a new task before completing the last, and he had little time for guiding and working with others. So we put him straight to work on our quiet days, Monday to Thursday, twelve hours a day, along with just one or two other front-of-house staff. It worked out perfectly. Steve had been doing ridiculous hours and so had we. It was win-win; he got time off at the weekends and we managed to get at least a little time off in the week. Meanwhile, Janine worked more with us at the start and grew with the business.

Over the eleven years, we had some lovely supervisors who came and went, such as Jo, Amy, Martin and Nick. However, it was Janine who, along with Steve, really committed herself to the Sun Inn throughout our ownership. They understood the role of host and 'owned' the place, filling our shoes when we weren't there. They both made a massive contribution to the overall success of the business. We were never quite the perfect employers we wanted to be and they too had their moments, Steve one or two more than Janine. But as a team we filled each other's shortcomings with trust and honesty and, most importantly, these guys weaned us off the seven-day week BLDs. For more than ten years, they provided the consistency and continuity of the business and most especially a welcome like no other. We are forever grateful.

From that first Saturday when we opened and Lucy and I stood outside the inn and looked in at 10pm with a full house, Lucy knew we'd taken on something much bigger than we'd anticipated. Her comment of 'what on earth have we done buying a pub' was quite telling. She knew from that moment that our business was going to grow exponentially and I'm not sure that her heart really looked forward to the prospect, but her commercial head certainly did. My head and heart were bathed in flattery and optimism. For that first year. Lucy and I would do anything and everything to make sure the business was a success. We were never sure if the business was driving us or we were driving it, and at times it was like riding a wild, untamed stallion.

Partly out of self-preservation and partly to play to each other's strengths, Lucy and I moved towards focusing on particular areas of the business. This was driven partly by necessity but increasingly to allow Lucy to draw breath and retreat to her comfort zone away from the continual demands of the operational side and to create a more organised and process-driven business.

Lucy's skills were definitely the ability to turn disorder into order. She was logical, extremely bright and very perceptive. Her birth father, before he died, had been a chartered accountant and although Lucy was not so good at maths in school, she really did enjoy the numbers side of the business. If the experience of running her own business taught her one thing it was that she should have had a career in accounts rather than sales; but the truth is she's talented at both.

With the continued growth in bookings and the rising number of people we were employing, office administration and finance required her time, leaving me to concentrate on the operations side of the business downstairs, together with maintenance and ongoing development projects.

We never articulated it or discussed it enough, but we both knew we were clearly in the early stages of moving from a small to a medium-sized business. Our first business plan before we opened identified no more than six employees and we were now up to between twelve and fourteen. Before a further two years passed, we would be up to thirty. Lucy and I found the mental transition from a corporate mentality to a small entrepreneurial family firm quite easy, but we now had to build infrastructure to deal with a far bigger business which we were slow to react to and which, as a result, brought new challenges.

We hung on to our new baby very tightly and made nearly all the decisions, as a result not fully allowing the team to develop and grow with the business, and leaving us under too much pressure most of the time. We simply did not devolve authority and responsibility as effectively as we could have.

On the flip side, some of the team members were not comfortable or ready to be made accountable and some could not make the transition; while others were losing motivation because we did not fully delegate. Looking back now, I think we never really bit the bullet on this aspect and it did hold us back. On the face of it, we both had the corporate experience and were used to much larger operations; but in truth we never really moved the culture and devolved responsibility sufficiently to do this. We had our opportunities on a number of occasions to force this through, once when we were seriously considering buying The Royal in Kirkby Lonsdale which was then a derelict building and again when we embarked on a team development programme. If we had bitten the bullet on either occasion we would have broken through this barrier.

It's relatively easy to take a business from A to B (from a pub to an inn) but much harder to take it from B to C (six to fourteen staff) and harder still from C to D (five-star inn and thirty staff); but to move to the next stage D to E, leaving it to a manager to run the show with a team of staff is even more difficult. We were far too close to the action physically and mentally and, to some extent, time was running out for me to take this leap. We had a good business and could retire in comfort in a few years so why risk it to grow bigger, creating a collection of inns? As for Lucy – well, she never wanted a pressurised job, just one she could enjoy. Don't get me wrong, we did develop the infrastructure enormously and the team to a certain extent, but our hearts and to some degree our bodies were not up to conquering that next step. As a friend once said to me, quoting the Peter Principle, 'In the business world, a person tends to rise to the level of their own incompetence'.

This ability to take an enterprise from small to medium-sized and then to a large business takes a great deal of mental strength. I so admire people like Lord Forte, who I used to work for and who managed to do this. He started out with one milk bar and ended with an empire of hotels and catering establishments. Moving from hands-on to strategic and from strategic to corporate governance takes a very strong mental shift.

In his first milk bar, he recognised that one of his staff could run the bar better than he could and he left her to it while he bought his next business. There were occasions when he realised that he could not afford the staffing levels he had and still make money, so he reduced the staff and left them to find a better way to do things; which they did. This example of icy-cold financial calculation combined with trust and belief in people whom he held to account with a firm grip, are the qualities of people who can make this transition. In Kirkby Lonsdale during our time there were two people who managed to achieve this shift. One was Fiona Robinson - and her dad - who started with a place a few miles away called Longlands and then opened Plato's in Kirkby Lonsdale and now has a third place; and the other is Richard Taylor, commonly known as 'Plug', who owns The Orange Tree in town. He went on to set up the Kirkby Lonsdale Brewery and now also has The Royal Barn. My hat goes off to both these people. Kirkby Lonsdale is so much the richer for them.

In our partnership, Lucy would describe me as the captain and herself as a very strong co-pilot. We both had firm views on all areas of the business and in the main we respected and trusted the decisions that we each made in our emerging designated areas. Often, we would discuss all areas together, but there was at times an uncomfortable undertone that I was making all the decisions. This worried me greatly on two counts. Firstly, because I knew I had this tendency to assert myself, so could be guilty; but most importantly because I truly valued Lucy's judgement. She made good decisions based on logic and understanding, and my assertive actions, whether perceived or real, meant we were in danger of losing all that we had achieved and, heaven forbid, Lucy withdrawing from engagement in the business.

Lucy's natural stance is to have time and space to look at all options, research, reflect and so on; whereas mine is make something happen soon or we could miss the boat. When Lucy's planning nature and my action nature were in harmony, we were a truly winning combination, but when we were not in harmony, much tension and frustration was created. As hard as we worked on this aspect between us, the pressure of the business with all its challenges and sheer exhaustion meant that we had our fair share of dynamic and explosive outcomes. This may have been one of the drivers to divide up responsibilities between us; but it mainly taught us that living over the shop that was operating 24/7 was not good for our health, or most importantly, our marriage. We both needed a little space and time to take on the relentless challenges. Both our batteries were running on flat by now and we needed time and a place to recharge.

As I write these chapters, it might seem as though everything fell effortlessly into place for us: the property coming back on to the market; the funding by the bank; a busy prosperous business, and so on. But I can assure you we really had to fight to make things happen. Some people say the harder you work the luckier you become; well that may be true, but the quote I often use and have embraced like one or two others I draw from, is one from Louis Pasteur that 'opportunity comes from a prepared mind'; and our escape from living over the shop would be just that. This next move also appeared to fall into place as easily as the ones before it.

We always had it in mind to convert the upstairs 'manager's' flat to guest bedrooms and move out, knowing what pressure it was living over the shop 24/7 with everything going on below. But that was about to change, thanks to a journey we made one bright sunny day in June 2007. We were travelling back from Kendal on the old Kendal road after a visit to our accountants - where we had just received a final copy of our first full trading year set of accounts and were feeling very proud – when we saw a sign saying lodges were for sale at Hawkrigg Farm near Old Town. Action man that I am, I said: 'Let's just go and have a look.'

Lucy was usually much more cautious, but the 'strike while the iron is hot' mentality came over both of us this time as we were so desperate to move out of the flat and have a home for ourselves. Well, the view from the farm was just stunning, right over the Lune Valley, and our reception from the Cowan Family who have farmed there for years, was wonderful.

They were diversifying from just farming into building lodges and, after a few pleasantries and a visit around a show lodge, we knew it was for us. By the end of that October we'd designed and commissioned a brand-new lodge with two bedrooms, bathroom, kitchen and dining lounge, all with magnificent views.

Funding came from our growing new business. To put it in to perspective, occupancy in the April of 2006, with just five rooms was sixty-two per cent; in April 2007, now with nine en-suite rooms was eighty-two per cent. So, to fund our new lodge we took out a further £100,000 loan from the bank against the business. This had to be repaid over the same period as the first, so we now had an additional £10,000 a year to pay in repayments and interest. It was a risk and the first of a few occasions when we had to watch cash flow like a hawk although future occasions would be due to spending capital on the business not our sanity. One of these future cashflow challenges would result in our getting help from an unlikely source, but that's a tale for later in these pages.

This move to the lodge made a world of difference to the way we both felt. It gave us time and space to think and most importantly relax in our own home, which we had been without now for nearly two years. We'd made the boundary crossing. The risk of selling our home and giving up everything we owned to become entrepreneurs now seemed to be behind us and the transition from being a corporate worker to running our own business had been successfully traversed.

# Taking on the Valuation Office

What you have to learn and understand about the hospitality business is quite amazing; and, like life in general, you never stop learning.

The rateable value of a property was not something I'd ever paid particular attention to and, besides, for the first few years all our energy was placed on developing the product and growing sales and profit. I thought rates were a fixed cost and one you could do little about.

However, we did receive unsolicited calls from organisations that made it a business to act for clients against unfair assessments of public house rateable values, claiming they could reduce our rates. On one or two occasions I was intrigued and took the opportunity to meet up with them. It's a type of no-win no-fee arrangement where the agents take about forty per cent of the first year's savings. I was keen to hear what they had to say; but I arrived at the conclusion that if we were to challenge our rates, forty per cent appeared high and I should do it myself. Having discussions with these agents gave me an insight into this world of business rates.

If Lucy had been present at the meeting, I am sure she would have drawn a different conclusion and employed these people. She would have taken into account factors such as time, experience, understanding, and so on. However, we did not pursue a rate reduction because our current rateable value figure at the time seemed OK and, well, sometimes ignorance is bliss.

Soon, however, we were to find we faced a shocking increase with worse yet to come.

Ratings valuation should be clear and transparent and, in a sense, it is. You can clearly compare the rates of other properties on the Valuation Office website and when you delve into your own ratings you can see how your rates are arrived at in their calculation. But this is where the straightforwardness stops and the injustice begins. Especially if you are growing sales exponentially.

There are two methods of valuation in assessing rates of hospitality businesses. One based on square metre and the other on something called Fair Maintainable Trade; that is, on the sales turnover of the property multiplied by a tariff. Restaurants with bars and restaurants with rooms are often based on square metres, as is much of the retail sector, whereas pubs and inns are on Fair Maintainable trade.

The reason for having two methods is not at all clear to me. Maybe it's a hangover from history; but it clearly favours the big brewers who offer tenancies, as the rent they charge tenants often reflects the rateable value of the property. So the higher the rateable value the higher the rent they can justifiably charge. In this way the harder the tenant works to build his business and grow sales the more is taken in rates and, therefore, rents. Eventually the tenant gets fed up as however hard they work to grow sales, the profit is taken away in increased rents and rates they have little control over. They give up the lease, often at a great loss, and move out. The building stands empty or a relief manager is installed until another unaware person embarks on the same journey.

We saw this on a number of occasions with the tenanted public houses in Kirkby Lonsdale. It seemed to go on a three-year cycle, just like the revaluation cycle. First year, lots of enthusiasm and growing sales; second year, realisation the rates are too high and an appeal begins. But the appeal process is so long, drawn-out and complicated, that the publican eventually gives in and by the third year gets out, leaving the rates set at a high level, justifying the norm for other pubs' rates to be judged by comparison. All very sad.

The Valuation Office tends to justify Fair Maintainable Trade by its being agreed by the British Beer and Pub Association. We were told by the representatives who wanted to claim reductions in our rates that this institution was dominated by the big brewers who own the properties, who, as we have already seen, have a vested interest in higher rates. I don't know this for a fact but have always feared it may be true. Whatever the cause, it's an injustice and I was quite incensed by not only the method of calculation but equally by the appeal process that I shall talk about shortly.

If you think about it, the building is a shell and has a value. OK, fair enough; but this should not vary according to the sales activity within this shell; this is the responsibility of the tenant or the business operator who pay tax both on sales – VAT – and on profits.

In our case, and I suspect in many other similar businesses, the financial outcome between the two methods of business rate calculation is very different. It can be double or triple, as was our case, if you are judged on Fair Maintainable Trade. It is, I believe, one of the biggest reasons that we have such a decline in pubs, which are one of our finest British institutions.

In our case, the rates valuation of £22K in 2007 moved to £63K in 2010 and in 2013 with the sales we were now making, was set to go to over £85K.

Before we took over the Sun Inn, the then Labour government reformed licensing hours, claiming it would help stimulate pub businesses. Instead, in my view they should have reformed the ratings valuation system to help our pubs, bars and hostelries to invest and grow.

A question the law does not define clearly enough is: when is a pub a pub? For instance, where there is a bar with a restaurant, is the property a restaurant or pub? Or, in our case, where we had a restaurant with a bar and rooms – is that a bar, a pub, an inn or a restaurant with rooms? Or how do you define a change of status, such as from a pub to a restaurant with rooms? It's very opaque. We all sell food and drink and should be valued on the same basis; that is, on the square-metre method.

There is such a great difference in the financial outcomes of the two methods of valuation when it comes to re-valuation, which is done every three to five years or so. The square-metre method of valuation of a property is simply calculated by multiplying the size of your property by a value per square metre. In this case, the size of property remains constant and, when revaluing, the rates are only adjusted by the value per square metre.

In the case of Fair Maintainable Trade (FMT), it is much more complicated. This is calculated on revenue; not just total revenue, but varying tariffs based on different revenue streams; for example, rooms, food and liquor. Each revenue stream has two or three different bands and each band has different tariffs that are multiplied by your turnover. So there are many variables – the tariff, the band and the type of turnover. Not only this, but they are then further assessed against a grey scale or spectrum such as the character of the building, the type of trade, and then finally assessed. Could you imagine a solicitor's office rates assessed against the revenue they take? On top of that, wanting to know the breakdown of type of work they are carrying out; for example, house conveyancing versus matrimonial work because one revenue stream may be more profitable than the other. It's outrageous, but there it is - two different ways to measure retail outlets, both selling the same goods and services. You will not be surprised to know that the more complicated method produces the highest rates.

In our case our appeal took eighteen months from 18th April 2011 until 15th October 2012.

We based our arguments on the information provided in the Valuation of Public Houses Approved Guide, which outlined ways in which variations of valuation are made. After a great deal of research and dedication to the cause, our arguments, in essence, were:

1.  The David Beckham argument. The guide states that fair maintainable trade is what is reasonably expected to be done by an ordinary tenant. We stated that if David Beckham ran the Sun Inn, it is likely that sales would significantly increase; however, this would not be the fair maintainable trade. We argued that our higher level of sales was exceptional, not because of the property but because of our skills, expertise and dedication to the business.

2. Compared with other similar properties in Kirkby Lonsdale, we were being asked to pay much more.

3. The percentage increase in the investment we'd put into the value of the building was less than half of the percentage increase in revaluation of rates we were now being asked to pay.

4. The slow speed and complexity of the appeal process fuels inflated rates for other public houses used for comparison as they give in to their new rates and leave without a fight.

5. Affordability: we demonstrated that the FMT method meant that we would be working below the minimum wage threshold and there would be no profit to re-invest.

6. Unfair competition: those properties valued by the square metre paid half the amount of rates of those on FMT and, therefore, could charge lower prices for the same value and gain market share uncompetitively.

7. When is a pub a pub? When is it a restaurant? When is it a hotel? We argued that we purchased a pub and turned it into a restaurant with rooms. The valuation officer was having none of this argument; but we felt we had a strong case here, especially with a competitor in town – Plato's – which was a restaurant with rooms and was very similar to our operation but fell into the square-metre method of assessment.

With these seven arguments, we went in to bat at the tribunal. By now, we had an A4 file full of evidence to back up the argument with pages and pages of charts and documents. It took us more than five weeks to pull our statement of case together because of the complexity. In addition, we had to compile numerous letters and correspondence just to get a pre-appeal, before we could make the formal appeal. You can understand why companies make a business out of this and many appellants give up halfway through.

As I've said, it took us eighteen months; but I'm sure it would have taken much longer had we not received help from our local MP Tim Farron. He supported our case and helped move it forward; as well as our constantly badgering the tribunal officials to speed things up. In that sense, the eighteen months could perhaps be described as a quick turnaround.

I would not have put myself through this were it not for my absolute outrage at the business rates injustice – not only the valuation but also the process. Thankfully, I was bolstered by Lucy's brilliance with the clarity, logic and order she applied to our arguments. Otherwise none of this would have been possible. On more than one occasion, Lucy said, 'Mark, why are you bothering? You can't beat the system.' This may have been true, but nobody was going to stop me having a go.

It's business operators who take all the risks to develop and grow their enterprises; and after all the effort, time, money and hard work they put in, their success pays the government more VAT on increased sales and more tax on profits. FMT is really an additional back-door sales tax – just so wrong. The tax collectors take none of the risk or put in any of the effort; they simply pluck the fruits of someone else's endeavour. Hopefully, now you can see why I wasn't going to give up, both on principle and for the financial security of the business.

I've already said our rates moved from a valuation of £22K in 2007 to £63K in 2010, and in 2013 were set to shoot to more than £85K. You can see the injustice of this system and the detrimental effect such a huge increase in rates would have had on our business.

This whole process cost us a great deal of time and money. The tribunal was in Manchester, where we had to stay overnight. After the first day of hearing with our long arguments and detailed analysis it was adjourned and re-convened in Kirkby Lonsdale at the town's institute, from where the tribunal chairman and panel visited the Sun Inn and numerous other hospitality properties in the town to help them assess our case.

During the hearing, the valuation officer was allowed to state his case after we put ours and we were then able to cross-examine him and challenge his arguments. This procedure happened in each location. It was like being a barrister in a courtroom, but with none of the training of a member of the legal fraternity.

Unbelievably, a few weeks later we were officially informed we had successfully challenged the unfair valuation. Not only had we got through the outrageous process, but the rating valuation was reduced by almost two-thirds, putting our business back on track.

Lucy and I are both grateful that we were given a little slack by the chairman of the tribunal who did observe it was very rare for owners or managers to ever come to a tribunal to represent themselves. That being the case, it's little wonder that so many valuations go unchallenged and the reason why other businesses they are compared to end up suffering the same inflated rateable values. Even more of an injustice is that you cannot claim costs against the valuation office for inappropriate valuations, so it is a huge risk that the appellant takes in challenging the rateable value at tribunal.

The other aspect to consider here, and I refer to it in the 'Return on Capital Investment' section, is that hospitality property values are often based on the profitability of the business. This is usually ten times the EBIT (Earnings Before Interest and Taxes) of profit. So, for every £10K of profit the business makes, the business (that is, the property, fixtures and fitting and goodwill) is worth £100K. So assuming our rates went up by a further £25k and reduced profit by £25K it would devalue the selling price of the business when we came to sell by a quarter of a million pounds. It was this that certainly grabbed my attention and, ultimately, why I could not let it go.

As at the time of writing this book in 2019 this same antiquated method is adopted for pubs and a different method for restaurants, restaurants with rooms where in fact they are all selling the same product and services as a pub.

# Marketing and Selling Rooms

Three or four weeks before completing our purchase from the previous owners, it was clear there had been a reluctance by the then relief manager to let bedrooms. However, Lucy and I felt we ought to try to secure some advance bookings or elicit enquiries to give us a headstart before we took the business on.

Lucy set up a basic enquiry form and a one-year diary with all the rooms laid out day-by-day, which we dropped off with the relief manager to capture some early bookings in the three weeks prior to handover. However, on the day we took over, we were very disappointed to find that not a single enquiry had been logged, let alone any actual bookings. The state of the bedrooms and the appearance of the pub would, in my opinion, have put many people off, but we couldn't believe that there had been no demand at all. On a positive note, sales couldn't get any worse and at least the only way was up.

At midday on the day of our arrival, we put up two large posters: one at each entrance door, saying we were closed for three weeks and explaining the new products and features we were creating at the inn. The following day, much to our relief, enquiries started to roll in.

Dear Customers,

We are very proud to be the new owners of the Sun Inn and would like to share with you our plans.

The inn will now be closed until 11th April whilst the first phase of redevelopment is carried out. This consists of:

- Redecoration of the bar
- Creation of a small lounge area
- Redecoration of the eight bedrooms
- New beds with pillow top mattresses, puffy duvets and loads of pillows
- Identifying and sourcing a selection of special easy drinking wines from around the world
- Putting in brand new beer lines ready to serve an excellent selection of Cask Ales from Jennings and other locally sourced breweries
- Providing fresh filter coffee in the bar area

Later in the summer the second phase of development will commence with:

- Replacement of the roof
- Renovation of the gutters and down pipes
- Painting the outside of the inn

We have appointed a new chef, David Ostle, who is in the process of preparing the kitchen and creating a new menu based on English and European dishes, sourced from a variety of local produce and served in a contemporary and informal style.

To help us look after our customers we are recruiting the following positions:

- A kitchen assistant (22 hours per week including weekends)
- Bar and waiting staff (5-12 hours per week including weekends)
- A cleaner (14 hours per week including weekends)

We would like to hear from any interested applicants who are friendly, reliable, caring, honest and who can help make the Sun Inn a happy, enjoyable and comfortable place to be.

For any enquiries or bookings either phone 015242 71965, email sun.inn@ or just ring the bell!

We look forward to meeting you when we open on the Tuesday 11th April.

Kind Regards,

*Mark & Lucy Fuller*

The first involved a block booking for five rooms for Whittington Races, a popular point-to-point in a nearby village, held at Easter. We felt we would be able to get five rooms, stripped, redecorated, refurnished and back to letting in time for the Easter weekend, in just over three weeks.

By the time we re-opened three weeks later, we had more than £5,000 worth of advance bedroom and restaurant bookings in the bag. It was our first piece of marketing: perhaps more public relations than advertising. It was very personal and conversational: more informative than a hard sell. The poster covered the whole door, blanking out the entrance. The customers couldn't come in, but at least they knew how to get hold of us and make bookings and, perhaps most importantly, knew who we were. To sell, you have to stimulate demand and this piece of print cost us very little, about £60-80, including laminating it to protect from rain. It certainly caught the attention of locals and visitors to Kirkby Lonsdale and was all the advertising we did prior to opening. It did the job handsomely.

Most corporates spend at least two to three per cent of sales income on advertising. Our piece of print alone came in at 1.4 per cent of the £5K of advance bookings and showed a fine return.

Throughout our time we never spent more than two per cent of sales on the cost of advertising, marketing and PR, apart from the capital cost of developing our reservations system. It's a relatively small amount of expenditure, but critical, and it had to be applied creatively and with great care in order to stimulate demand.

Room sales is all about stimulating and managing demand. It was touch and go whether we could manage our demand and finish the bedrooms for letting before we opened the restaurant and bar; but I was determined we would open the newly created inn with letting bedrooms in order to 'cast the die' on the business model that we were going to operate right from the start.

We never planned to run a pub, just a bed and breakfast, but couldn't find a suitable property. What attracted us to the Sun Inn was the potential to create eleven en-suite rooms in an idyllic location. We purchased the business with nine letting bedrooms – two double rooms with baths, two double rooms with a shower and five rooms sharing one bath and two toilets. Each of the bathrooms were pretty grim with sixties-style avocado and pink bathroom suites, cracked tiles and mouldy grouting.

Stage one of our bedrooms' redevelopment was to strip out all the carpets, furniture and fittings and simply clean the bathrooms and decorate throughout eight of the nine rooms. We remodelled the room layout and bought super new beds with pillow-top mattresses and the new headboards made by Lucy's dad.

We re-carpeted and furnished with side tables and dressing tables, again made by Lucy's dad; while wardrobes were purchased from IKEA. To change the bathrooms and make all the rooms en-suite was a big cost and, as we had not yet fully understood demand, we felt it unwise to make such an investment at that stage.

Over time, however, we did invest, heavily, and converted all rooms to en-suite with new bathrooms. With the conversion of the manager's flat, this meant we ended up with eleven letting rooms.

Because we kept improving the standard of accommodation and setting a price tag to match the quality, we must have changed our customer base at least three times over the first six years. We started selling the rooms at £45 and ended up charging £130-£160. We started from zero per cent occupancy and raised it annually to more than eighty-five per cent. All this was achieved by stimulating and managing demand in order to maximise room occupancy and sales. Perhaps it all sounds easy, but it takes a lot of management time and know-how, in which Lucy and I to a certain extent were well versed.

The rooms element of an inn is the most profitable area of the business. At its height the accommodation represented approximately thirty per cent of the sales and seventy per cent of all the overall profit; whereas the food and drink represented 70 per cent of the sales and only thirty per cent of overall profit. So you can see why I was so determined to publicise and let the rooms before we opened.

The food and drink side of the business was definitely the most demanding aspect in terms of our time and attention. We could have focused all our effort on this but remained disciplined, and concentrated at least half our management time in developing the rooms side of the business. Don't get me wrong, food and drink were key elements in attracting residents, so we could not ignore this aspect; but our level of attention to detail in the management and development of our rooms' business was ultimately what delivered profit and realised the value of the building.

Our second print order was a very valuable marketing tool: a small A4 threefold brochure. We quickly had this produced once we'd opened and commissioned new photography. The important aspect of this brochure was to get over the attention to detail of the overall product and demonstrate the charm of the building. Well-shot photos were essential and the first shoot cost us around £600. The pictures lasted a couple of years until the next phase of development was complete and they became outdated; but these photos were used extensively on our website and other mediums.

We were very careful not to spend too much on our first run of 2,500 brochures (believe me, it's easy to get carried away to produce an over-the-top glossy one). The brochures were strategically placed and were often picked up by guests who came for a day visit to Kirkby Lonsdale. A significant number would call in to have lunch or dinner and subsequently come back for a short two- or three-night stay. The brochures flew out the door and our print run went up to about 3,500 each year.

In our early days of running the inn we were told by 'marketing specialists' that printed brochures were old hat now and not required with the advent of websites. However, I would balance that advice with an awareness of your customer profile: websites are an excellent way of marketing a business but not all age groups adopt them. Even at the end of our time at the Inn, with the advent of social media, smart phones, interactive websites and such, these brochures were still a key tool that attracted new visitors, as many people enjoyed browsing them when they popped in for a drink or a bite to eat and then learned we had bedrooms. Needless to say, we always ensured the brochure boxes were full, and anyone showing interest in our rooms would be rewarded with a tour of the rooms, which made a great impression and often converted the sale.

Critically, we recognised how important it was that we charmed our guests at lunch or dinner as it greatly impacted on a day visitor returning to stay for a short break. Lucy and I led this charm offensive early on and the staff quickly followed. It was our view that the welcome and the happy atmosphere was fifty per cent of the product; the other fifty per cent was the food and drink and the charm of the building. It was always about getting close to our customers and understanding that they wanted to feel like VIPs and were being personally looked after.

In any hotel, inn or bed and breakfast there are two types of accommodation markets – leisure and commercial; and within each of these two groups there are many sub-groups. We knew it was important to differentiate the different approaches when it came to stimulating demand and marketing to one or other of these two groups.

For the leisure market you have to do a lot more marketing and PR. This includes telling people about any awards you have won and creating interesting stories about your property to capture people's imagination in newspapers, magazines and other publications. Whereas for the commercial sector, you have to go out and directly sell to organisations, establishments, agents and contacts, often on a one-to-one basis in order to stimulate demand.

In this respect, we were in a bit of a dilemma early on as we were not sure exactly what sort of mix of business we were going to attract and, therefore, what our approach should be.

Our hunch was that the split would be around sixty-five per cent leisure and thirty-five per cent commercial. However, after the first few months it was clear leisure demand was ninety per cent, so that was where we focused our approach when it came to stimulating demand.

The sub-group of leisure guests we attracted were couples and individuals and not groups, who would often want discounts. Also, the size and the number of rooms meant the Inn wasn't a natural fit for groups. Importantly, leisure guests were considerably more profitable than commercial guests. This was for three reasons:

a)   There were usually two people in the room, which meant two lots of drinkers and diners;

b)   They tended to stay longer – that is, two or three nights rather than one and, therefore, there was only one linen change and reduced costs; and

c)   Their budget was not restricted by a commercial boss. It was their leisure time and they wanted to spoil themselves, which often would involve some sort of celebration where they wanted to splash out for something special. In this respect, we were always conscious that we needed to demonstrate and market that 'something special'.

The exposure from getting an article in the right magazine or newspaper is quite amazing. Four years into our ownership, having developed most of the bedrooms, we were lucky enough to have an article in one of the national Sunday newspapers. Our phones went crazy with bookings and continued that way for months, such is the power of that medium. However, to attract this kind of article took a lot of pro-active PR and a clear strategy in the way we marketed our rooms.

Having spent all that energy on stimulating demand, a key part of our approach was to secure repeat customers. That process began with the initial enquiry and the welcome at the front door. It was our philosophy that, at the initial inquiry, we were entering into a relationship with the customer over a period of years and not just focusing on the booking they were placing that day. It was just like a first date where we were looking for a long-term relationship and not just a one-night stand.

Guests would be greeted with a heartfelt welcome at check in, with a handshake, eye contact and an introduction by name from someone with a kindly disposition who was going to take the time to look after them. They would attend to the guest's luggage, help to navigate the challenges of parking, take them to their room and explain all they needed to know to quickly orientate themselves to the room and the building.

It was all part of the training regime we installed, undertaken by all our staff before any of them were let loose to check in guests. Lucy picked up on an idea early on to extend this home-from-home sort of feeling and allow guest to feel like they belonged with us. This involved not only complimentary tea and coffee in the room, but also from the bar at any time throughout their stay.

This provision, which was clearly mentioned as part of the check-in procedure, added a warm and generous value for our guests and, in truth, was of little cost to the business. Indeed, it helped to grow sales as the guests went straight to the bar where, more often than not, the lady had a complimentary tea or a coffee and the gent a well-deserved pint, which certainly was put on their bill. Or perhaps they would both have coffee and then quickly slip into a glass of wine and a pint they would not have had otherwise purchased.

All this careful handling made a good first impression and stimulated positive feelings about the inn, putting guests into a positive frame of mind. For repeat customers, we also included a small bottle of fizz and a personal 'welcome back' note.

These were some of the simple and low-cost but high-value techniques and approaches that we used to achieve a thirty-four per cent return rate. In other words, four out of eleven rooms were filled each night by guests who had stayed before; and many would stay three or four times a year. Unlike many corporate organisations, we would spend more on adding value for the guests in terms of goods and service and less on marketing to attract new guests. To further engender loyalty, we would always follow up a stay with a thank-you note and three times a year, would send a conversational newsletter. This informed our guests about new products, services, matters of interest as well as any special offers we had to fill our trough periods.

Looking after our regular guests and continually communicating with them throughout the year was an important part of our business growth. It sounds simple looking back, but at this time not many businesses were doing it. Even now as this sort of thing is the norm, the difference is – and was then – that we did it with love and care. Now it often feels just like a 'process' when you receive such messages. Processes are an important part of a business as we will look at next; however, the customer should never feel they're part of a process.

# Creating Order and Systems

Early on, Lucy introduced some set office procedures and processes to ensure we maximised on rooms revenue and projected a professional and warm approach; but it was paper-based and very time-consuming. We had both come from corporate hotel backgrounds that had sophisticated and detailed computer reservations systems to optimise room sales, so for our paper-based system we had to go back to basics.

As the volume of reservations grew, we knew we needed some sort of computer-based reservation system but were conscious that we had a relatively small stock of bedrooms to sell. Also, our employees were all very multi-skilled and many of them part-time, so there was little point in introducing a complicated system. While we looked to see what the market could offer, we decided we could afford the luxury of a part-time reservations coordinator and the first person to take this role was Shannon.

Shannon, a lovely Irish lady with a soft and caring manner, was the fiancée of our head chef Sam. During the day she did housekeeping and in the late afternoon and early evening she would do reservations and check-in. She had never done this type of work before and took to it like a duck to water with her calm easygoing friendly manner along with her methodical organised approach. Customers would love the fact that she had talked and corresponded with them in advance and then on the day checked them in and made them feel so very welcome and at home. The advantage of working in housekeeping as well as reservations was that she knew all the rooms intimately and her product knowledge was superb.

We recognised early on just what a success she was at converting enquiries into a sale. Her combination of calmness and listening skills together with her friendliness and great product knowledge, meant that she was able to gain confidence with the client, make recommendations and close the sale. At both enquiry stage and check-in she set the scene for the guest throughout their stay and her caring follow-up letter when they left often clinched a return visit. Don't get me wrong; we had to get it right for our guests throughout their stay, but the major impression is often made within the first seven seconds and that's what we worked on.

Another factor here is the Sir Isaac Newton rule: 'For every action there is an equal and opposite reaction'. If we were really good to our guests, our guests would be really good to us. And so they were in every way: very friendly and accommodating with the staff, generous with tips, and happy to extol our virtues on social media. Of course, the reverse was also true and occasionally we had to reinforce our philosophy with members of staff who lost their way on this.

Shannon's taking on and growing this role, allowed Lucy more time to spend on marketing and PR and, most importantly to secure an appropriate computerised reservation system that would take the management of our rooms to a new level while keeping it simple for staff to operate and straight-forward for customers to use online.

When Lucy and I left the corporate world, online website bookings were only a small element of the business, around three per cent of bookings being transacted this way. We were certain this was a growing market and a business opportunity and that it must feature strongly in our new system. Lucy researched high and low to find one that was appropriate; not over-complex, but able to deliver on basic rooms management techniques, data capture and seamless movement of deposits from the customers on making a reservation to our till on the day of arrival.

At the same time, we were looking for something to replace our old-fashioned till in the bar, handed on from the previous owners, which was hard work to use and impossible to interrogate for management information. In effect we wanted both jobs to be completed by one piece of kit. There were such things on the market but they all came with a level of complexity and sophistication that was way above our needs and very time-consuming to master. It would be like a sledge-hammer trying to crack a nut, with a cost to match.

It was probably a reflection at the time of the size of the market for our sort of product. The market has grown hugely since then, as have computerised reservation systems. Back then we were able to find the level of sophistication in the tills but not combined with a reservation system. Finally we accepted that we couldn't buy a suitable combined system, and instead we chose a new till system from a local company LCR in Morecambe who were keen to work with us to 'connect' their system to a reservation system should we be able to find a suitable one. Lucy took the bold step to work with our website provider, a local software company Big Fish Internet Ltd (BFI), and design our own bespoke reservation system.

The whole system took more than one and a half years to build and bring to fruition. We produced a detailed brief and specification which Lucy masterminded and I chipped in with. However, breaking new ground is not always straightforward and it took twice as long to programme and cost a load more than the original quote we were given. The team at Big Fish were great and absorbed the cost of the extra work and we were cool about the over run on time. Working with two other local firms like this to make a brand new product felt very exciting. We'd worked for corporate companies; we were running our own business; and now we were working as a collaboration. This was new, exciting and dynamic.

We introduced the new system just, alas, as Shannon was leaving us. Losing her was a blow, but a double-blow to lose her husband as well, our head chef Sam. Tragically, Sam's mother Bernadette had suddenly passed away and the family felt they had to move to back to London, where Sam hailed from, to start a new life. Bernadette was a lovely person and it was a shock to the family, to us, and judging by the number of people at Bernadette's funeral at Lancaster Cathedral, to most of Lancashire as well. We hold dear to our hearts the lovely times we enjoyed her company at the Inn; but it was the end of one era and the beginning of another.

Shannon's legacy lived on as other special people took over her role for the next seven years, most notably Sarah, Charlotte, and Hannah. Each of these were cast from Shannon's mould, but amazingly all three brought something new to the party. Sarah elevated the role to a full management position with her skill in communicating; making the office the hub of the business and forcing us to begin holding departmental meetings and uniting an ever-growing team. We set financial targets which she always managed to achieve.

Charlotte helped move our website forward and introduced us to working with social media, and Hannah combined the Office Manager role with a greater connection to operations and incredibly, held a full-time job while completing an MA in Clinical Counselling at the same time, no mean achievement.

The importance and reliance we placed on the role just grew and grew and became a key managerial role within the business. Eventually, Lucy and I had to move out of the office and build a new one for ourselves, to allow both the reservations management role to flourish and to create an additional desk for our accounts administrator, Natalja. Back in Latvia, where she hails from, Natalja had worked as a professional book-keeper in a construction company. When we took her on as housekeeper in 2008, we had no idea about her background. Often you look at staff only in one light, but many employees have exceptional talents in other areas; and it was a joy to Lucy and me to discover this new talent within the business who could support Lucy in the accounting arrangements. She carried on as head housekeeper as well as helping with accounts which gave a useful insight into how her consistently high standards in the rooms converted into profit in the accounts.

Funnily enough, when we interviewed Natalja, her command of English language was quaint to say the least and at the interview she did not wait for us to offer her a job but said in her heavily accented Russian: 'Aye hev decided aye em gon wok for you.' How could we refuse? It would be the start of a long and happy relationship. Since then, Natalja's English has come on in leaps and bounds, although thankfully it remains quirky.

It was wonderful to see such hidden talent flourish and was possibly one of the most satisfying dimensions of the business that Lucy and I were keen to nurture with all our staff. Natalja took on the role of part-time book-keeper as well as housekeeper and, after a short while Natalja's daughter came to work for us, too. At first Arina could speak very little English, but she was a marvellous worker, and very quick to pick up craft skills. At times she would work in the kitchen as well as in housekeeping and often would be faster and more exacting than others who had been working longer in those areas.

Some staff worked for us for a long time before going on to be a doctor or an architect. One loyal member of staff Joelle worked for us for the entire eleven years, starting while she was at school and continuing during university holidays; and even after she became a trainee solicitor, she would often work on Christmas Day for a couple of hours in housekeeping. I think many staff felt like family and often liked to return.

Implementing the new reservation system was a new challenge; it forced us to completely review our existing systems and processes as you can't force a computer system into an existing one, and so a new process has to be built around it. The booking element of the system was embedded into our website together with a large bold 'Book Now' button; and this moved online reservations from ten per cent of bookings to more than thirty per cent.

The system, and the revenue growth it brought, presented its own challenges. All the work force had to adapt and take on this new technology as the business reached another level in its development. With our paper-based arrangement, we had only one diary and one person taking a reservation at a time. Now with this cloud-based reservation system we had unlimited access to our diary. This meant that instead of taking reservations one at a time and having to call back people who had enquired, we could now take reservations in the office, and downstairs, and even have the phones diverted to our home and take reservations there as well.

Managers could interrogate the bookings to assess advance bookings for doing rosters, or for housekeeping to look at special requests or the number of stay-overs compared to arrivals. As a result, we had to train many of our staff to handle the reservations, and quickly realised we were asking a lot more from people who were previously used to just serving food and drink or servicing rooms. Some were comfortable with the challenge and thrived on both the training and taking reservations; others were deeply uncomfortable.

Rostering had to take account of at least one member of staff other than the manager who could take reservations and check in guests during the evening to that same standard as Shannon had set. This meant more training manuals had to be written, training carried out and then coaching to perfect staff skills in the new role. It wasn't just training the staff but growing their product knowledge as well.

Lucy's reservation system not only brought a new level of sales but forced us to grow the number of staff and their skill-set. Once it had been bedded in, Lucy presented back to Big Fish to show what a good system they had built for us and the difference it had made to our business, and she suggested they sell it on to recoup the money they lost on building it for us.

They understood the computer-programming business, but not hotels or rooms management and asked if we would like to form a partnership with them so the system could be sold to other hospitality businesses. For the past few years, that's exactly what we've been doing and there is now a portfolio of clients in the north west who are using the system, which we called Direct Room Sales.

# Cumbria Tourism

Leaving the security of a large corporate organisation and going it alone, as I have said before, comes with a number of risks. One of these is the absence of business support to draw upon to help develop and grow the business. You have to rely very much on your own skill and expertise, and inevitably there are gaps in your knowledge and understanding of what is new and happening in the market place. To help plug this gap we joined the county's tourist board, Cumbria Tourism (CT).

Known as a destination management organisation, CT was funded by a non-departmental public body, the North West Regional Development Agency, as well as by contributions from its members, of which we became one.

Tourist boards were set up all over the country to support popular visitor destinations such as the West Country, the Peak District, the Yorkshire Dales and, of course, Cumbria. Over the years, I did have some involvement with a number of them as I moved around the country running various hotels for corporate organisations; but, like all such organisations, you often only get out what you put in. In the absence of any other commercial support, Lucy and I embraced this organisation and they helped our business enormously.

If you ever went to any of their member meetings, you would think the organisation was run very poorly. Members often voiced complaints about what the board was doing or not doing or whether it was spending money unwisely in the wrong areas, but so far as we were concerned they did an awful lot right. I couldn't write this book without acknowledging the excellent support and help that CT gave us in growing and developing the Sun Inn. Soon after we joined they were offering a scheme called Profit through Productivity which would assign us a business adviser to help us look at our business for opportunities to improve profit, all for the highly subsidised sum of £90.

Our assigned business adviser was Gary Lothian, and we took to Gary as soon as we met him. A Scot in his mid-thirties with a soft accent, sharp and disciplined mind, he was immensely personable and engagingly supportive. He quickly identified opportunities for us to focus on in order to improve the profitability of our business.

These opportunities were all in important areas that had slipped by us as we worked eighteen hours a day, seven days a week. We'd been too busy looking after customers and not taking enough time to look after the rest of our business as we should have. It was to some extent a little wake-up call. The business was profitable, customers were happy and occupancies were good; however, hidden in the haze of the day-to-day activities, there lurked the opportunity to move our business up to a new level of productivity and therefore profit, to set us and the business on a new trajectory or growth curve.

The first area was our website. After only fifteen minutes of Gary showing us other fine examples of websites, we could instantly see in which areas ours was missing the spot. As a result, we rearranged the way our website was laid out to make it more user-friendly; we included pictures of each of our bedrooms so guests could see the room they would be getting, and we presented compelling reasons to visit the surrounding area, such as the stunning landscapes, the walks, places of interest and local activities. Most importantly, we introduced a bright orange button with 'Book Now' on the front page that took you straight to the booking page.

That was just the start. We began to look at statistics showing which part of the website guests looked at or did not look at; how many looked and then booked or did not book; and then how people were searching for the Sun Inn on the general web, were they looking for b and b's, inns, accommodation, restaurants with rooms and so on, and how many other establishments we were competing during a search.

This was all part of website optimisation and we were learning fast. We looked at other distribution channels such Cumbria Tourism's own distribution channel Go Lakes, and examined many others to see which were successful and which were not, signing up where we saw an opportunity. When we started looking at these distribution channels we saw one that we were getting a lot of hits from called Doggy Pubs which unbeknown to us, Janine the assistant manager who loved dogs had put us on. It was a free entry and the start of a niche that we carved out for ourselves in the marketplace and for which we won awards.

Opportunities can often stare you in the face before you twig, and the approach to dogs was just one of those. It took a number of other shoves before the penny really dropped and we started to focus on this market opportunity, adapting our product to be much more dog-friendly. In the end we believe it gave us a premium of at least ten percentage points of occupancy, over and above the market.

Digressing a little here from Gary's work, it's important to make two points. Firstly, you must get into the detail if you are going to fully understand your business and, secondly, when getting into the detail, always look for those small golden nuggets that are signs of vast new streams of wealth and opportunity to tap into like our golden nugget relating to dogs.

The instant success that Gary opened our eyes to was on the pricing of our rooms. Firstly, he helped us expand our horizon to look at our competitor set, not just locally but more regionally, examining both product and price. He made us reflect on our own success and the high occupancies we were achieving, especially at weekends, to demonstrate a supply-and-demand opportunity. We were cautious about this at first because we always wanted to ensure value for money and not rip off customers, for the long-term success of the business. But it became clear that we could increase prices by at least another eight to twelve per cent and still provide great value for money. We could have left the prices as they were, but we moved on to discussing with Gary how we could refine our product to our customer profile.

If we increased our prices, this would return more profit to reinvest in the product, enabling us to further improve our standards for our customers to enjoy. Up went the prices; to our amazement, there was very little evidence of resistance, whether verbally from our regulars or through any impact on our occupancy levels, which actually grew.

This led to further work with Cumbria Tourism on customer profiling, and Mosaic profiling our database. By the time we came around to profiling our customers we had about 2,250 on our database, each with a postcode. What Mosaic does is profile customers into a large range of types or categories, partly linked to age, wealth, affluence, influence, background and occupation. From extensive research, Mosaic can extract a profile from the type of neighbourhood the customer lives in, and hence postcode. You may have heard terms such as empty nesters (parents whose kids have left home, often leaving more money to spend on themselves) or Dinks (double-income couples with no kids, that is, cash-rich and time-poor).

Well, Mosaic uses a large range of categories like Corporate Chieftains, Golden Empty Nesters, Captains of industry. Each group is intimately described: its likes, lives, aspirations, needs, and so on. The idea is, if you understand your customer base intimately you can attract guests by offering a product to the exact specification they desire. With this insight you can refine your product accordingly.

When your guests are profiled with this system, you not only learn what different range of profiles you already have but also how many more of one type of profile there is against the national average. In other words, the type of guest that is more naturally already attracted to your style of property. Our type of customers wanted a hundred per cent assurance of a great experience. They wanted to know the details of quality: not just a comfortable bed, but a bed with a pillow-top mattress. Not just fresh linen, but Egyptian cotton. Wine glasses made from crystal. Where the food was sourced, the breeds of animal used. These were experienced and discerning customers with wealth to match. Not arrogant or flashy or overly experimental – they just knew what they wanted and wanted it delivered in an informal and friendly manner, first time, every time.

Gaining this clarity of insight over our customers helped us enormously in tailoring our product and ensuring we described it accordingly on the website and in printed material. It also helped in the recruitment, training and coaching of staff to ensure they understood the level of detail and understanding that was required.

When we came to the next development: converting the manager's flat into three new en-suite guest letting bedrooms and gutting our kitchen and toilets to create modern up-to-date facilities, we realised early on that we would run short of cash. While we were happy to borrow money, we did not want to over-commit ourselves. Lucy said what we needed was a grant, and she'd seen something about one in the Cumbria Tourism's newsletter.

The Tourist Boards facilitated European Tourism grants, and the one Lucy saw was called Tourism Connect Grant. The advert was asking for tourism businesses to apply for a grant of up to forty per cent of a total development project up to a maximum amount of £60,000. To qualify, the project must grow tourism in the area, benefit the local community and be environmentally considerate.

With due haste, Lucy completed the application form and sent it off to see if we might be eligible. Amazingly, within fourteen days our application was successful and we were told we could formally apply for a grant. So began a frantic six-week dash to put a business case together that met the exacting standards of the grant in time to meet the closing deadline.

Europe being Europe, these standards were detailed and long-winded. We had also been tipped off that there was a limited pot of money so there was an element of first-come-first-served about it. However, the quality of the application did have a huge bearing on success.

Completing the outline business plan was a worthwhile exercise as the one we had written to purchase the Sun Inn and carry out the first plan of changes was now complete, and this gave us the direction and clarity to create a true 'destination inn'. We called the plan Driving for 5 Stars, as our ambition was to create a 5-star guest accommodation inn with an AA rosette restaurant.

The most challenging part of the plan was setting out tenders for building work and obtaining quotes as well as obtaining planning permission on our Grade 2 listed building. There was also a lot to do to include environmental benefits, growth in staff numbers and training and development arrangements as well as the benefits to the wider economy of the region. It was touch and go as to whether we could turn the plan around. Lucy did her magic and laid it out clearly and succinctly with drawings, pictures, words, quotes, and documents; and, if needed, she would have put it all to music as well!

Eventually we submitted the application for a grant of £57K on a £144K spend. We decided to leave the upgrade of the toilets out of the equation as we had already reached the level of the maximum grant so it was unnecessary to commit to that at this stage.

The document was duly sent off by recorded delivery on 13th June 2008. We expected to wait for weeks before a reply but on 27th June we received a formal letter offering us a grant for the full £57K. We both were delighted and frankly quite shocked, not believing that for all our hard work over the six weeks crafting that document, we could earn £57K to invest in our building. We both had smiles on our faces a mile wide that day.

The offer was not without conditions: if we sold the business within five years we had to pay back a proportion of the grant. Also, for the next three years we had to report monthly on the outputs of the project so that they could be evaluated. Nevertheless, it was a great outcome and we got on with the work from that September and finished by the following January, 2009.

The final area in which Cumbria Tourism supported us was public relations. They had a PR department to promote the whole region and often when journalists wanted to do features and articles on the Lake District, they put us forward. The pitch was something like: 'You normally turn left at Junction 36 of the M6 to go to the Lakes, but why not turn right and see some equally stunning views of the Lune Valley.' Turner's and Ruskin's links to the landscape and so on were mentioned and, of course, the quaint seventeenth-century Sun Inn. It seemed to do the trick and capture the imagination. But when the development agencies were disbanded during the credit crunch, the organisation could no longer fund these services. Instead they set up a commercial arm with a bespoke PR agency run on a purely commercial basis, which suited us perfectly; we used this service for many years as a major part of our strategy for marketing rooms.

CT arranged for many journalists to visit the Inn from around the UK, including London; we often had guests telling us that they saw the Sun Inn advertised in the *Newcastle Chronicle* or *Liverpool Echo*, and so on, or many other local and regional papers. Even my friends in California, Terry and Aileen, would tell us about articles they had read locally over there.

So there you have it: a terrific organisation giving us business support, insights into our business, a £57K grant and wide-range PR exposure. It is a tribute to Ian Stevens the then chief executive and all the board who made this happen during the time we owned the Inn.

Lucy did put a little back into the organisation. She was selected for their management committee and sat on it for more than three years, but this was nothing compared to the amount of support we received from them. For this and everything they have done for the region we say a very big thank you. We are convinced they not only helped us but also helped the town, enormously.

# 16

# The Kitchen and Sam our Head Chef

We had five head chefs during our time at the Sun Inn. One who only lasted days; one under a year, and two over a year. Then there was Sam, who was with us for eight years. They all greatly helped us but somehow other aspects of life got in the way for them at some point or other, as it does for all of us. We had the utmost respect for all these guys. Second to our role, it was the most challenging in the business.

The kitchen is the boiler house of the hospitality business and if that goes out or dies down it affects the whole operation. In our case it operated from 7.30am right through to 11pm, seven days a week, like a roaring fire for much of the day. We only closed for a deep clean on Mondays between 10am to 3pm, so no lunches were served on that day. Breakfast merged into lunch preparation, then lunch service, which merged into dinner preparation followed by dinner service. It was relentless, physically demanding, and time critical; and was totally reliant on hundreds of successful transactions of goods and orders throughout the day and, of course, people – customers, staff and suppliers. You just needed one of these factors out of synch and you could quickly get into trouble, as we often did! It was a case of always being on top of things.

Fresh food has a very short shelf life. Order too much and your profit is wasted. Order too little and you upset customers. It's a fine balance, and a chef's life is often lived right on the edge for much of the day.

The reputation you have spent months and years building can be trashed overnight with a health scare from either a customer or an environmental health officer with an improvement notice, or worse, a closure notice on the front door or bad publicity. So cleanliness, temperature control, cross contamination and the provenance of fresh food is critical at every point of the day and every stage of production. Apart from ensuring these are right, you also have to prove it by keeping accurate up-to-the-minute records.

Second to wages, our chefs controlled the biggest spend in the entire business. This spend was made up from many different items of ingredients. Each day there could be six to ten invoices with twenty to forty different items listed, the prices of which could vary depending on time of the year and availability, as well as between different suppliers. To tie down suppliers was not as easy as you may think and fluctuations needed to be carefully monitored.

Then there is the technical skill in creating and cooking dishes that are appealing and at a price point for your market and being able to deliver these consistently every day and in a very short time frame.

I think you get the picture. A highly pressurised environment, requiring great attention to detail, complete dedication, and a special type of person with strong leadership skills.

There were times when we were without a permanent head chef and relied on agency staff. It was at these times we were most vulnerable. The food gross profit goes out of the window, cleanliness often drifts and standards can become inconsistent. For some chefs it can all get too much. Some just walk out, some get so stressed that they shout and ball out other members of staff in a most aggressive and abusive manner, and some go off the rails with drink and drugs. So thank goodness that for almost eighty per cent of the time we were at the Sun Inn we had Sam as our head chef who created a stable and happy environment.

Sam's career had started early the hard way as a kitchen porter washing dishes, pots and pans and being pulled in to peel vegetables when short of staff. He quickly showed interest in cooking with an ability to match and was soon working as a commis chef. He worked in a number of good restaurants in the UK, Ireland and Italy, before joining us as sous chef, or second chef, to support our head chef at the time.

It was touch and go whether he was going to join us or Hipping Hall which at the time had rosettes and accolades for its food, with an excellent reputation to match. Afterwards Sam said the reason he joined us was because he liked our energy and dedication and the direction we were taking the business.

When recruiting, it is not often you selecting a candidate, but a candidate selecting you; a fact that is easy to forget. The way you handle each stage of the recruitment process can say a lot about an organisation. Unfortunately, Lucy and I often found ourselves far short of the mark in this regard with the many demands placed on us each day.

Fortunately, Sam chose us, with the added bonus of his then fiancée Shannon who joined soon afterwards, whom I have already mentioned. Sam immediately fitted in with the kitchen operation and when John our head chef left it seemed quite natural to promote him to the role immediately.

Lucy and I felt we had a special bond with Sam, one of mutual respect and understanding. What we lacked in knowledge, he had, and vice versa. We pulled together in the same direction and supported each other for the benefit of the customer and the business. We all learnt as we went along on the journey.

Our ambition, Sam's and ours, was to obtain an AA rosette for our food, an accolade and distinct mark of quality that no one else in Kirkby Lonsdale held at this point.

We purchased one day of consultancy with the AA for an inspector to help us with this ambition. We took him through our current dishes and talked through our plans for our new kitchen. He held no punches as he tested each dish – perfectly polite but brutally frank. He could taste a bouillon stock from a homemade one from five hundred paces; flavour combinations at first taste; technical skill at the first slice. The only item we received praise for was a French apple tart; even then there were question marks over the exactness in cutting the slice.

He recommended that Sam should go on a further one-day course to fully understand what the inspectors were looking for in both one, two and three rosettes and other awards such as a Michelin star. So off Lucy and Sam went while I held the fort.

At one stage on the course they were both blindfolded, noses clipped and asked to taste various foods to test their palate. We probably taste with our eyes and our noses more than we rely on our palate and it was their first lesson. Taste is so important; don't rely on looks and smells. They had to retrain their palates; for Lucy a novice, and Sam, a smoker, this was a salient lesson and possibly one of the reasons why he gave up smoking. Much of the day was spent on flavour combinations, texture combinations, food provenance in terms of local sourcing and seasonal variation. Most importantly, what does technical skill look like to an inspector.

That day made a turning point in our food and set Sam's and the team's cooking to a new level. Back came the inspector months later for a new food tasting, with a new menu and a new kitchen to match. We were all nervous. This time Sam sat in the restaurant with the inspector and the team had to cook and present each dish without Sam's intervention. A good move really as it's all about consistency, even when the head chef is not there. The team got it ninety per cent right. We tweaked the dishes ever so slightly leaving things out rather than adding anything ensuring we did not detract from the core flavour.

We were now deemed ready for formal assessment and were put down for a mystery visit. These occur every other year, when you are a member of the AA, to check the service and facilities and the quality of the food to form the overall grading. Eventually a pair of inspectors came to dinner, which we had not expected as a single inspector normally comes either for an overnight and dinner or just for dinner. The next morning, they came back, and carried out their routine inspection, and were kind enough to put us out of our misery before they checked over the rest of the Inn. We had achieved the one-rosette level, which gave the whole team a real boost for weeks to come, and was a great marketing tool to use to attract new leisure business, with some great PR.

I've already mentioned Sam's departure for two years. You never quite realise what you've lost until it's gone and it was such a relief to hear Sam was coming back to the area and interested in returning to the Sun Inn. The break and the experience he gained from his time in London gave him a fresh impetus and even more confidence. We quickly gained a two-rosette standard from the AA and we rebranded the restaurant Carter's at the Sun Inn to reflect and recognise the following that Sam now had for his food.

He had the ability to build a loyal team, and over the years we were lucky enough to have some very loyal and talented kitchen staff. Charlotte, who was Sam's sous chef, took over from Sam when he departed for London. She was a good cook, technically superb and very detailed, almost obsessively so, getting incredibly stressful if anyone didn't follow her lead.

She did have a fun side. On Sunday mornings at about 8am, she would arrive after a tiring Saturday shift the day before and demand a cup of tea. This fell to me as I often used to run the restaurant for Sunday morning breakfast. There would be Charlotte getting Sunday lunch ready, while Angela, another great character, would be cooking the best breakfast I'd ever experienced in more than thirty years in the business.

They were both very strong characters and very demanding about their tea. I always tried to lift the mood by insisting they sing me a ditty in order to get their cuppas. It went something like this:

'I like a nice cup of tea in the morning,
I like a nice cup of tea with my tea,
And about this time of night,
What goes down a treat you are right
Is a nice cup of tea.'

It always did the trick; from 8am to 10am those ladies worked like Trojans, laughing, joking and talking away as fast as they were producing wonderful food.

Then there was Luke Whittle. A lovely lad. He spent two to three years at Kendal College gaining his culinary qualifications as well as working for us, and then joining us full time. Luke was like a child protégé, definitely head chef of distinction in the making as he produced dishes that were exacting and precise, especially in the pastry section of the kitchen. Although he operated at a moderate speed, what he lacked in urgency he more than made up for in quality and reliability, and somehow he always managed to complete his work. Unlike another character, a chef called Andy, who most people referred to as 'chopper', who was fuelled by Lucozade and other similar sugary-stimulated drinks. You could not hold him back. In fact, he became so hyper at one stage we had to have words and wean him off them.

Chopper was a fun guy who mostly loved to laugh and joke; but he was hard working and loyal, doing fourteen – fifteen-hour shifts if necessary and he'd always be there ten minutes before his shift the next day. He had a penchant for limericks and often got carried away laughing and singing so loudly that the guests in the restaurant on occasion would ask: 'What's all that about - a young lady from Devizes? What's the chef singing?' I never told them always hoping they hadn't heard the full version. He was a colourful member of the team, a one-hundred per cent asset; occasionally a one-hundred per cent liability, but most people loved him for it.

Johnny, one of our kitchen porters, gravitated to trainee chef and was often in charge of making our fresh bread. He, like Sam, had great talent, but like all young lads would occasionally be led astray, and it would be our responsibility to get him back on track. I knew his career could work out just like Sam's and it was great to have Sam as a role model for him. I must say he made great bread, which often took twenty-four hours to prove and bake; he certainly had dough fingers to pull off this mark of quality.

There were many characters who worked in our kitchen, too numerous to mention here, who all worked bloody hard and long hours and to whom we were truly very thankful. There was a clock prominently placed on the kitchen wall above the hotplate and progress was measured against every quarter of an hour to see if you were ahead or behind before service. When checks start to fly in with orders, you have to be fully prepped with all your 'mis-en-place' or prepared items of food at the ready to quickly cook and put a dish together. To turn a main-course dish out in ten to fifteen minutes means there can be no errors. Everything has to be in place, just like a production line. There is no second chance to get it right without delays to customers so the pressure is always on.

After a busy shift, with your adrenalin flowing, you are mentally and physically exhausted. We know this as occasionally Lucy and I had to roll up our sleeves and get stuck into cooking breakfast or prepping veg. Getting stuck in the kitchen though is dodgy. As owner/manager you can quickly neglect the overall business and things start to slip, so we were blessed having Sam who took good care of our engine room for so many years.

We were further blessed by Sam not only encouraging his wife to join us working in housekeeping and the reservations office for a time, but also his Dad who worked on the bar. Their presence made a real difference to many aspects of the Inn. In some respects they were like our relatives, always very encouraging, supportive and kind.

# 17

# The Charm of the Church Bells

The ring-a-ding-ding of bells have followed me around most of my life and brought me good fortune and happiness. Being born within the sound of Bow Bells; Dad's calling as a vicar and the bells of his church; grandfather clocks at my grandparents; and the sounds of Westminster chimes on the mantelpiece at home must have provided a subliminal sort of comfort and security for me. So it was very apt that our first business venture of running an inn should be right next door to a tenth-century church with a Norman tower and a fine set of bells. It kind of felt right somehow and may just have been the intangible element that gave us that gut instinct to buy the Inn.

The bells of St Mary's Church have been ringing for centuries heralding births, deaths and marriages, celebrations, remembrances and, of course, calling folk to worship. Outside these events the church bells chime out the time of day and close by there is a sundial that also measures the time by the sun's direction, but in a much quieter fashion. In fact, the Sun Inn was named after the sundial that was a landmark locally called 'the Sun'. The original sundial can be found inside the church; the one in the churchyard opposite the Sun Inn is a replica.

For many people in Kirkby Lonsdale, the bells of the church have been a constant feature; they have grown up with them, they're very much part and parcel of the rhythm of their daily lives, night and day. But for some guests staying with us, who were either insomniacs or just light sleepers, the ding, ding, ding, every quarter of an hour and the bong, bong, bong every hour with the number of bongs depending on the time of day was like the drip, drip, drip, of water torture being applied in the prison of their bedroom cell late at night and in the early hours of the morning.

As I've said before, sleep deprivation is a well-known form of torture, and, on occasion early on in our ownership, a light sleeping-guest would set up court next morning in the breakfast room; they as prosecutor and I the accused for allowing such torture. Other guests looking on would be the jury while the prosecutor laid out their case about the night-long noise of the church bells. The jury by now would be well into their bacon and eggs, but conversation halted while the drama unfolded. Finally, the case for the prosecution, eloquently and forcefully presented was over and eyes were upon me to put the case for the defence.

Running breakfast on my own I had half an eye on guests entering the restaurant, who needed to be greeted and seated, and half an ear open for another familiar bell from the kitchen signifying the next cooked breakfast was ready to go out from the kitchen.

In this demanding and challenging moment I endeavoured to apologise and explain what an ancient monument the church is and what little control I have over the ecclesiastical working of the diocese to prevent the holy clock from chiming all through the night. The defence was not convincing. Unfortunately for us the same scenario was being played out to the world now on Trip Advisor by other customers and we quickly realised we were being sentenced with bad publicity, a turn-off for anyone contemplating staying with us. Action was needed and needed fast and a solution found before the judge of social media condemned us to bankruptcy.

We could not stop the bells so we concluded that the answer lay in throwing money at the problem by double-glazing windows in parts of the building and secondary-glazing in others. This was complicated by the fact that we were a Grade 2 listed building; everything we did required planning permission and listed-building consent, and that involved drawings and visits by officials and so on before we could get contractors in to do the work.

Eventually, after vast expense and delay and more comments by customers the works were completed to the windows that faced the church or were adjacent to it. Problem solved, or so we optimistically thought.

Sound is like water, it seeps through the smallest of gaps and vibrates off tiles in the roof into our top-floor rooms. Yes, an improvement, but the problem had not been solved, especially on warm nights when guests had their expensive double-glazed windows open. We could not get free of guest comments about the bells even with all the effort and cost that we had put in. It was truly depressing.

Lucy and I were both in the office when one of the regular church-bell comments pinged through on an email from a recent guest and Lucy, at her wits end said to me, 'For Christ's sake!' – quite appropriately I thought as it was the church causing the problem – 'Why can't light sleepers use bloody earplugs like I do?'

Of course, we would not have dreamt of saying that to a customer, but it did show the level of frustration that we were experiencing. A seed, however, had been planted in my mind: why not get earplugs for our guests? Good idea! But to bluntly leave earplugs at the side of the bed to cover the problem of the bells would almost make matters worse and draw attention to the problem. However, like many things in life, it takes a little thought; and like the song, 'It ain't what you do it's the way that you do it; that's what gets results', we set to task with the idea, sourcing a small, beautiful wooden box with a hinged lid for each room, and inside the box we put two sets of ear plugs. On the lid was a brass plaque engraved with a note saying

*For snoring partners and*
*The charm of the church bells*

Dad made the boxes, and the brass plaques came from Taylors across the road. An amazing shop is Taylors, it sells almost every type of hardware and much, much, more: passport photos, knives, handwarmers, torches, boot and shoelaces, coats, hats, beer, paraffin, lamp oil – you name it, they have it or can source it. Such a great asset for the town and a great tourist attraction in its own right. The earplugs, which we purchased in the hundreds, costing just pence, came from Screw Fix.

Anyway, unlike our first attempt, throwing loads of money on double-glazing, the church-bell complaints evaporated immediately, and the church bells kept on ringing, as they had done for centuries. To our amazement, we even started to get compliments coming through with guests saying things like: 'The Inn thinks of everything, they even provide earplugs, which was useful as my husband always snores when he has had too much to drink.' And this on Trip Advisor: 'Don't worry about previous comments about the bells, I did not hear them and even if I did, they provide earplugs in a charming little box beside the bed.'

For us, this was one of those examples that demonstrates that throwing money at a problem is not always the answer as often there maybe a better cost-effective solution. The good fortune and happiness of bells in my life had been restored. The words of my old mate Dave Skinner, came flooding into my head yet again, when after his third or fourth pint and bottle of Sancerre in hand, he's say: 'Ring a Ding, Ding.' This time it was heard with even more gusto.

# 18

# Accounts

'Know your numbers' was the first of the ten commandments insisted on by a managing director I used to work for. Previously, I'd worked for Forte Hotels, where you were only as good as your last month's profit and loss account. Needless to say, both organisations instilled a great awareness of numbers in me. Knowing numbers is one thing, but actually doing your own accounts is quite another, especially if you want to comprehensively drill to interrogate the data.

Double-entry bookkeeping, journals, nominal codes, prepayments and accruals ledgers, debits and credits is not a world I feel comfortable in, so Lucy taking all this on was a great relief. Don't get me wrong, I took a healthy interest in our numbers once completed but putting them into the Sage accounting system in the right order and in the right department code was not up my street.

Lucy has a wonderfully logical mind and the ability to quickly turn disorder into order. Fortunately, she never missed a payroll or a VAT return, and with her bank reconciliations any slight errors were picked up at the end of the month.

Lucy just loves numbers, she can turn them upside down, back to front and whatever format you want them in; many of our financial controls and our comprehensive analysis were a direct result of her numerical ability.

Latterly Lucy went back to college and gained some formal qualifications, which she much enjoyed. I'm certain that her timely compilation of a whole array of numbers was a major contribution to our financial success and always guided us on our journey. I shall talk more about that in the next chapter, Controls.

We were introduced to a firm of accountants then called Lonsdale's, now called Moore and Smalley, by our solicitor and family relative Allan Garrick. From the very first point of contact to way after the sale of the Inn, this organisation served us brilliantly and wrapped its protective arm around our business, adding value at every stage.

I remember my first phone call with Michael Proudfoot, a partner with then Lonsdale Accountants while standing in the car park of the corporate hotel where I was general manager. I wanted clarity on many aspects of handling accounts and setting up of a new business. I suppose my torrent of questions would have seemed to Michael like a river bursting its banks during a storm. But his patience and calm style on the phone helped calm the inclemency. He was reassuring that everything could be taken care of in the time-frame, also about the expenditure involved in registering a business, and so on. What struck me about Michael and gave me the gut instinct that this was the man who was going to help us look after our business interests was the care, time and patience he took both in my phone call and during our first meeting. It was not so much about what Lonsdale's could do for us; it was all about understanding our circumstances, our goals and ambition.

Our first meeting was hurriedly arranged for 7am early the following week, which meant we were out of our house near Chester by 5.30am to make the appointment up in Kendal. With luck we could be back in our corporate office and hotel by 10.30am without arousing any suspicion. The previous evening, we did not get to bed till after 12.30am as we wanted to finalise our numbers and projections and had only managed four hours' sleep. However, the adrenalin and excitement of our adventure and the chance to create a brand new life, escaping from the 'Colditz' of a corporate life, kept us alert and feeling very much alive.

Michael escorted us to a meeting room and we quickly got down to our business plan and projected numbers, anxious to get his considered opinion of these. He listened intently and his questions were delivered in an encouraging manner. You could see that his nature was cautious. He interrogated and considered everything very carefully. His assessment of our numbers was made early on – not that you could tell as he patiently allowed us to travel through our setup costs, initial expenditure, sales projections and expenditure as well as the market opportunities. What Michael was weighing up was tax and cash movements, two areas that our minds were nowhere near. In hindsight they really should have been.

You see, in Michael's mind he was searching for ways he could help us build up cash quickly to re-invest and breathe new life into the Sun Inn to release the potential of a repositioned business. He knew about the property and a little of the history of the previous owners and you could tell he had much more belief in our ability than (perhaps) we had at this stage. I'm certain he saw it immediately as a good opportunity. He also realised the key to releasing the full potential of the building and our business was always going to be in carefully thought through capital investment to properly reposition the business. And this needed cash.

Michael's first recommendation was to complete three first-year budget scenarios; a worst-case and best-case in addition to the antic-ipated case we'd presented to him. From all three he wanted us to see cash flows for each potential outcome. He thought our projections were conservative, which appealed to his cautious judgement. He felt we were likely to do far better; but, in any case, by showing the worst-case we would be able to see for ourselves that we could still fund the project. He also realised that we had not taken account of the benefits of a positive cash flow that this business was going to generate in the early months. You have probably heard of the term 'cash is king'; well, when running your own business, the treasury function of managing cash is just so important and an area we had not been fully exposed to before. For each scenario he insisted that he should produce for us a cash flow to match.

What Michael was keen to demonstrate was that we were going to have a cash-rich business as our sales were either in credit card or cash on the day of sale. There was no sales ledger to manage or anything like that. Our costs (purchases) were not going to be due for payment for least twenty-eight days, or three months in the case of VAT; so, we would have a pot of money available early on for re-investment. We did have a £100K overdraft facility from the bank for investment if needed, at a cost of three per cent interest, it was best avoided. What Michael wanted us to get a fix on was exactly how much cash might be freely available dependent on how successful we were in the first year.

The second area that Michael was weighing up, and one we were oblivious to, was the most tax-efficient type of business that we should register; that is, a limited company, partnership, limited partnership, and so on. We were and still are very ignorant about such matters, except we now know that depending on your circumstances it can have a sizeable implication on the amount of tax you have to pay and tax you can claim back.

Our understanding from Michael at the time was that a partnership, as opposed to a limited company, would allow us to offset an annual loss in the current year against the last three to five years of tax payments. So in our case, if we made a loss in the first year we could claim a refund of tax against the tax we paid while in our corporate jobs.

Michael's questioning over the exact dates we were taking possession of the pub and exactly how long we were closing for while we cleaned the building up and re-presented it as an inn were not really obvious at first.

He later explained why timing really does matter. If we were to take possession of the pub at the beginning of March and briefly trade with a sale or two and then closed for a few weeks while we carried out a large amount of maintenance spending on the fabric and contents of the building, there would be a considerable tax advantage. By 4th April, the end of the tax year, we could declare a large loss for the first year of trading. This loss could then be used to claim back from the tax Lucy and I paid the previous year while working for our corporate employers.

I thought, wow! Could this be true? If so, it would be a great move and was simply wonderful advice. Michael further advised on the merits of a partnership for claiming back capital expenditure, which was not so favourable for a limited company. As we were eventually to spend over £600K on capital, it sealed the deal on the type of business to register.

We did review our position with Michael and another tax expert from their company some five years in but concluded that a partnership was still the best option to continue with. In some ways, it also summed up the relationship that Lucy and I had: 'A true, open and equal partnership with each other, drawing on each other's strengths to the common good.'

So in one phone call and one meeting, Michael had found for us £22K from a tax refund and a further £35K of working capital. We put that to good use after eight months of trading when we created three brand new deluxe rooms and replaced the hot-water boiler that had by this time been condemned by British Gas.

These additional new rooms provided new revenue streams for the business, which in turn started to finance our investment programme for other areas. After that there was no looking back. It was Michael who helped us get the cash rolling and set us on our way.

He visited the inn a few times to review our progress and on occasions brought his wife for lunch to check out the business from a customer perspective. He was always on hand for advice and support outside of the annual year-end adjustments, audited accounts and tax returns. As he came towards retirement he gently, over a number of months and maybe even two to three years, handed over the account to Colin Johnson. It was just the sort of style in which he took care of his clients and which had impressed me so much in the first two weeks of our meeting.

It was around the time that Colin was getting involved with our account that Lonsdale's merged with Moore and Smalley from Preston, coinciding with us starting to think a little about our end-game. We had always said openly that we were going to run the Inn for ten years, until I reached sixty, and then check the energy and engagement levels and most probably retire around then. Funnily enough, customers and locals were always interested in these matters and I often felt they were worried about what they might lose if we left. I was always sure they had a lot to gain from a fresh pair of eyes and a fresh dose of enthusiasm, but there you go.

Anyway, to head off speculation, we kept to our original ten-year script whenever a rumour did the rounds that the Sun Inn was up for sale, which, I have to say, did occur quite frequently. As part of the exit strategy, we were introduced to Lee Salter, a young man like Colin, with bags of nervous (but very informed) energy to talk about pensions, investments and life after the Inn with a financial plan to match. Colin was more of a rugby sort of a guy; solid and dependable and where Lee was a squash player, fast and tactical. They both worked well together with our financial affairs. It soon became clear that getting out of business can be as hard as getting into it, needing planning and careful navigating around the pitfalls that at first are not obvious, while also working out the costs.

When you buy or sell a business like ours, there are three elements to the overall sale price. These are building and plant, fixtures and fittings, and goodwill. When you sell the business, each of these elements is treated differently for capital gains tax. In our case, as we were planning on retiring, there is something called entrepreneurs' relief that may be applied to the physical building and goodwill element that can reduce the tax from forty per cent down to ten per cent. However, the fixtures and fittings remain at forty per cent. So it was in our interest to ensure that fixtures and fittings was a small element of the overall sale price, which took careful financial planning over a number of years to achieve.

Once you have sold and got the cash from the sale, where do you invest it? These are all challenges that can take a number of years to think through and plan for until you feel comfortable, and for this you do need expert advice; even so, it's a tricky business, and these guys are still looking after us now that we have begun a new life for ourselves.

My philosophy is that in the hierarchy of business, customers and the market should come first, closely followed by staff. However, accountants come a very close third. Back in my corporate days, general managers were often heard to say about accountants; 'They know the cost of everything and the value of nothing'. My view is that they know the cost and the value of everything and if you have the right ones, as we were fortunate enough to have in Michael, Colin and Lee, they not only know the value but also know how to add value (more of it) to your business.

# Controls

While the accounts show you the results monthly and annually of all your effort in numbers, it is the daily and weekly controls which guide you to ensure you end up with good numbers for all the hard work you put in.

Unlike some other businesses, hospitality is very much a 24/7 - morning, noon and night - 365-days sort of business. Staff and managers often work like ships passing in the night, by the time one member of staff has had two days off and the other member has had two days off, there are only three days that they might work together on the same day. Even then they may be working on different shifts. So communication is a serious challenge. Issues on one day can so easily drift to the next and, before you know it, a problem escalates and gets out of control.

For this reason, we knew how important it was to have systems, procedures and controls built into our business.

Our emphasis was to concentrate on selling rooms while controlling food and drink costs. This is because rooms are a totally perishable commodity. You cannot sell yesterday's un-let room today, so you must go all out to sell each day's rooms in advance or on the day. In contrast, food and drink stock has a short shelf-life but you can still sell it tomorrow or not even order it in the first place. In this way you are able to control the cost of food and drink.

Our other theory was that if you filled the rooms, sales of food and drink would take care of themselves with residents' dining.

After wages, food costs were our biggest expense. Fresh food is a perishable commodity and the fresher it is the better the quality. Using up all the fresh food on the day, or certainly by the next day, is essential otherwise it can literally be thrown in the bin. If you do this you may just as well throw the profit in the bin. Believe you me, this does happen. So the control of food costs, the second biggest after wages, is one aspect that can make or break you.

One way of controlling this is to introduce a 'shopping basket' system of control.

**Shopping Basket Example**

| Supplier | Mon | Tues | Wed | Thur | Fri | Sat | Sun | Total | % mix |
|---|---|---|---|---|---|---|---|---|---|
| Cheese larder/Butter | | 16·75 | | | | | | | |
| Udales | | | | | | | | | |
| Dales | 10·55 | | 10·20 | | | | | | |
| Lakes Speciality Food | | | 40·39 | | | | | | |
| Cartmel Valley Game | | 20·25 | | | | | | | |
| Johnson an swr | 30·45 | | | | | | | | |
| TOTAL MEAT | 41·00 | 37·00 | 50·59 | | | | | 128·59 | 29·9% |
| | | | | | | | | | |
| C&G Neve | 27·10 | 23·20 | 16·80 | | | | | | |
| TOTAL FISH | 27·10 | 23·20 | 16·80 | | | | | 67·10 | 15·5% |
| | | | | | | | | | |
| Wellocks | 31·39 | 27·40 | 42·16 | | | | | | |
| Oliver Kay | | | | | | | | | |
| Borders | | | | | | | | | |
| TOTAL VEG & DIARY | 31·39 | 27·40 | 42·16 | | | | | 100·95 | 23·5% |
| | | | | | | | | | |
| Mcclures | 30·03 | | | | | | | | |
| Turners | | 28·50 | | | | | | | |
| Oil Solutions | | | 33·60 | | | | | | |
| Mediterrea | | | | | | | | | |
| TOTAL DRY STORES | 30·03 | 28·50 | 33·60 | | | | | 92·13 | 21·4% |
| | | | | | | | | | |
| Lovingly | | | | | | | | | |
| Crema coffee | | | 20·79 | | | | | | |
| Bakery | 6·82 | 7·20 | | | | | | | |
| Petty Cash - booths etc | | 2·10 | | | | | | | |
| Petty Cash - booths etc | | | 4·71 | | | | | | |
| TOTAL OTHER | 6·82 | 9·30 | 25·50 | | | | | 41·62 | 9·7% |
| | | | | | | | | | |
| | | | | | | | | | |
| Purchases Daily | 136·34 | 125·40 | 168·65 | | | | | | |
| Purchases Cumulative | 136·34 | 261·74 | 430·39 | | | | | 430·39 | |
| Food Revenue Daily | 350·00 | 400·25 | 591·10 | | | | | | |
| Food Revenue Cumulative | 350·00 | 750·25 | 1341·13 | | | | | 1341·13 | |
| Gross Profit Cumulative | 213·66 | 488·26 | 910·74 | | | | | 910·74 | |
| Gross Profit % | 61% | 65·1% | 67·9% | | | | | 67·9% | |

The daily check to ensure food gross profit is in line. In this case by Wednesday it has achieved the required 68% GP

It works on the basis that you assume there is a level par stock of food in the kitchen that stays the same, so whatever food you purchase that day should be sold that day.

The minimum food gross profit that the chef needs to make is around sixty-eight per cent, which means that the food cost for each day must be no more than thirty-two per cent of the sales.

Every day, the chef enters the cost of purchases from the invoices on to the shopping-basket control sheet and at the end of the day or the next morning he/she enters the sales of the day (less VAT, of course).

In this way, each day the chef on duty can total up the purchases and work out the food gross profit for the day to ensure they were hitting this very important margin on a daily basis.

Some days the margin will be hit and others it will not, depending on whether the chef has purchased just the right amount of food for the forecasted business of the day.

As the figures are inputted day by day, you get a cumulative result as well as a daily result. In this way you can see that if you have over-ordered one day and ordered less the next, the cumulative position of at least a thirty-two per cent cost for the sales may still have been achieved. If, however, you are out of line for a few days and over-ordered each day, it is likely that some food is out of date and your profit literally is thrown in the bin. The shopping basket approach provides a warning sign to the chef about what's going on while also forming a great basis for discussions between managers and the kitchen team.

Our experience was that whenever this system was applied we nearly always hit our required food gross profit. But on the occasions we did not, the shopping basket system of control either flagged up a cost issue where suppliers had increased their costs without advance warning, or an expensive mistake by one of the chefs had led to food being thrown away (not unusual with trainee chefs); or it indicated that food signed for on the delivery note had not actually been delivered. Whatever the challenge, the important thing was that the issue flashed up after a few days and did not go undetected until the end of the week or, even worse, the end of the month when you run a full profit and loss account. I know from bitter experience that this can all too easily occur.

Food costs are notoriously difficult to control, but the ten to fifteen minutes spent on this shopping-basket approach each day can save hundreds and thousands of pounds. A sixty-eight per cent food gross profit can easily go down to fifty-eight per cent, and at this point the profit on food sales would convert to a loss after all the other expenses are taken care of. All that hard work and effort by so many people just to make a loss does not bear thinking about, so this sort of financial control is essential.

Perhaps the greatest aspect of this control system is that it is driven by the chefs on the shop floor and is not lost up in the accounts department. After using the system for a few weeks, the chefs get a real financial feel for where the food gross profit is at any one time and are constantly analysing and managing the food costs as they go about their day.

You will see that the control sheet splits the food invoices into specific areas so that at the end of each week the chef can compare with the previous week's total. He or she can see how much has been spent on dairy, meat, fish, vegetables or dry stores each week; if one area is higher or lower than the previous week, it may indicate where the problem lies.

Chefs don't normally like numbers, being much more interested in what is on the plate. But both aspects are essential and the shopping basket is an easy way to keep the finances on track.

Liquor is not such a perishable commodity as food, although beer quickly goes out of date and even before then loses its brightness. The liquor gross profit, like food, has to be maintained at the right margin; but the difference here is that the prices don't tend to change as often as food prices and, when they do, the suppliers tend to tell you in advance. Also, on most occasions the barman, unlike the chef, does not have to create the product but simply pulls or pours. For this reason, we only carried out full liquor stocktake once a month.

However, every day we did monitor wine consumption against sales. The routine is that when taking a drink order you put the order on the till and then dispense the drink. Quite often the restaurant manager or host would be the person with experience and knowledge of wines who would normally serve the wine. Sometimes the restaurant would get so busy that when a guest asked for another bottle of wine, there would be no time to place the order in the till before serving it. The intention to go back later to pop it on, however, is easy to forget, and I can say this as I was sometimes guilty. So each day we had a control sheet which we would complete with an opening stock of all the bottles of wine ready for dispensing and a closing stock to see how many of bottles of each wine had been consumed. This was then compared with the sales on the till register.

We often caught that bottle of wine that had been left off a guest bill at the end of the night. If it was a resident, it was easy – we just popped it on their bill. But if it was from a non-resident, we often had their telephone number and had to make that dreaded call the next day with an apology and an appeal to their good nature. On most occasions the customers were very good about it, but it was not something we wanted to make a habit of.

As well as an annual budget, split down month by month and compared with the actual month's profit and loss account, we also completed a weekly flash report.

I compared this flash report to the dials on the instrument panel of an aircraft. It told me if we were on or off course and by how much, monitoring each financial calibration of the week's journey.

This document, which Lucy produced every week, also showed comparisons with previous years; without it, we would have been running the business blindfold. You can see Lucy's creative use of numbers that not only show margins, sales growths, occupancies, yields, costs and gross profit, but also customer-service levels of appreciation by monitoring tips paid by customers. It also helped address issues of staff holidays, ensuring enough were being taken each week and were spread evenly throughout the year.

None of these controls are rocket science; in fact, they're all pretty basic. But it's the religious application of the controls day in day out, week by week, month by month, that is the key to landing the financial results that you are looking for.

# Weekly Flash Report

| | Last Year Wk 1 | This Year Wk 1 | Last Year Wk 2 | This Year Wk 2 |
|---|---|---|---|---|
| Rooms Sales | 7,400 | 8,100 | 6,890 | 7,980 |
| Food Sales | 8,680 | 8,875 | 7,230 | 7,130 |
| Liquor Sales | 6,790 | 6,371 | 6,030 | 6,700 |
| Other Sales | | | | |
| **Total Sales** | 22,870 | 23,346 | 20,150 | 21,810 |
| Food cost | 2,785 | 2,670 | 2,467 | 2,150 |
| Food GP% | 67.9% | 69.9% | 65.9% | 69.8% |
| Liquor cost | 2,050 | 2,107 | 1,874 | 2,040 |
| Liquor GP% | 69.8% | 66.9% | 68.9% | 69.6% |
| **Total cost** | 4,835 | 4,777 | 4,341 | 4,190 |
| FOH wages | 3269 | 3412 | 3306 | 3467 |
| FOH wage % | 21.1% | 22.4% | 24.9% | 25.1% |
| Kitchen wages | 3144 | 3456 | 2983 | 3251 |
| Kitchen wage % | 36.2% | 38.9% | 41.3% | 45.6% |
| Rooms wages | 657 | 746 | 773 | 735 |
| Rooms wage % | 8.9% | 9.2% | 11.2% | 9.2% |
| **Total Wages** | 7,071 | 7,615 | 7,063 | 7,454 |
| **Wage %** | 30.9% | 32.6% | 35.1% | 34.2% |
| **Gross Profit** | 10,964 | 10,954 | 8,746 | 10,166 |
| Rooms Available | 56 | 56 | 56 | 56 |
| Rooms Let | 52 | 50 | 46 | 51 |
| Occupancy | 93% | 89% | 82% | 91% |
| Lunch Covers | 300 | 280 | 210 | 230 |
| Dinner Covers | 228 | 213 | 198 | 210 |
| Total Covers | 528 | 493 | 408 | 440 |
| Average Spend Food | 16.44 | 18.00 | 17.72 | 16.20 |
| Average Room Rate | 142.31 | 162.00 | 149.78 | 156.47 |
| Rooms Yield | 132.14 | 144.64 | 123.04 | 142.50 |
| Housekeeping wages per room | 12.63 | 14.92 | 16.80 | 14.41 |
| Kitchen wages per cover | 5.95 | 7.01 | 7.31 | 7.39 |
| Tips per cover | 1.37 | 1.50 | 1.61 | 1.14 |
| Tips as %age of sales | 3.2% | 3.2% | 3.3% | 2.3% |
| FOH Hours | 347 | 331 | 351 | 318 |
| Kitchen Hours | 333 | 297 | 316 | 292 |
| Rooms hours | 74 | 89 | 87 | 90 |
| **Holidays Used - Target 11 days per week** | | | | |
| FOH Holiday days taken | 3.0 | 5.0 | 4.0 | 5.0 |
| Kitchen Holiday days taken | 4.0 | 2.0 | 3.0 | 5.0 |
| Rooms Holiday days taken | 5.0 | 1.0 | 4.0 | 0.0 |
| **TOTAL HOLIDAYS TAKEN** | 12 | 8 | 11 | 10 |

\* please note figures are examples only.

When things go off-course, they can do so very quickly and it is down to management intervention to set things right. This can sometimes be a quick fix or at other times, like an oil tanker, take a lot longer to turn around. You can use this weekly flash to monitor week by week whether the ship is starting to show signs of changing course or if more management action is necessary early on. It's no good waiting for the monthly profit and loss account to find that the ship is going in the wrong direction.

Controls can often feel like a negative instrument to show shortfalls in performance or to beat people up with, but actually they should be used in quite the reverse way. They should be a positive safety net to catch a problem early on, and more generally as encouragement to show that the business is going in the right direction. For all sorts of reasons, and as a result of all manner of distractions in our complicated hospitality business, it's so easy to take your eye of the ball and then, as they say, 'shit happens'. So we tended to accept this and use the controls to focus, keeping on the right flight path. We saw them as an encouraging sign, enabling numbers to be constantly nudged back into line to maintain our course.

We also had a number of other controls in the sales office to measure the pick-up of room sales, market share, demand and suchlike. These were equally invaluable to the profitable running of the business.

There is a saying: 'What gets measured gets done.' We most definitely used that approach in all aspects of our business.

# Funeral Teas

Nothing is for ever and, sadly, death is inevitable; well, probably at least in my lifetime, but who knows where science and technology may lead in keeping us all alive.

My dad, the vicar, thought philosophically about death. He felt natural death was a cleansing process for life with the next generation coming through much fresher and slightly better adapted to the future challenges this world presents. I'm sure that in grief philosophy like this goes out of the window, but he held this view right until his own death at the age of ninety-two and, in some ways, I am sure this approach helped softened the sadness of his passing and helped him and us, as a family, come to terms with the inevitable.

In a small community like Kirkby Lonsdale, you seem somehow to be much more aware of death than in larger towns and cities. Everyone seems to know everyone within the town and word soon gets around. St Mary's Church, next door to the Sun Inn, carries out roughly thirty funeral services each year and we became very aware of the number attended by locals with black ties and dark clothing passing the Inn on such occasions, paying respects often to people we had recently served.

Sadly a number of regulars who became friends passed away during our eleven years. It was a sobering experience and always reminded us of our own mortality and the importance of enjoying life to the full while we could. Dave, Fletch, Bernadette, Danny, Norman and Marnie, Debbie and both her parents, and Peter are but a few of the very special people we grew to be friends with, many of whom passed away before their time.

As a rule, we did not close our restaurant to block bookings or events such as weddings or social occasions. Our view was that you either ran a restaurant or a function room. If you dabbled in both using the same room, you were neither a restaurant or a function room and customers would become confused. On the very rare occasion that we closed the restaurant for a special event, we always received grief from restaurant customers turning up on spec and being bitterly disappointed. While we may have made a little extra money on the day, we believed this was short-sighted and to the detriment of the overall success of the restaurant.

Some funerals, however, took place between 3pm and 6pm in the afternoon, outside of our regular dining times when the restaurant was normally closed. Funeral teas would provide a welcome source of extra revenue, but I always felt slightly awkward making profit from someone else's loss or sadness. By their nature, funeral teas are always last-minute affairs and often unpredictable in their numbers, with the deceased person's family often part-organising the event from afar. They come to visit the Inn with a grieving husband, wife, daughter, son or other next of kin to finalise the arrangements. I always liked to personally take care of these enquiries both out of respect and to ensure that we could handle the number of people with the style of catering that was appropriate in terms of budget, expectation, content and logistics. These factors could on occasions be tricky to navigate around our small restaurant operation and for the kitchen between lunch and dinner service.

With the church next door, we received our fair share of these funeral teas. Some members of the team sometimes considered the £6- £12 food charge per head a small return for all the effort, but I was clear that it was an important service to the community and should be handled and considered appropriately. While we never catered for funeral teas with profit in mind, we did also benefit from additional revenue from those extra people from both near and far who popped in to the Inn for a coffee, drink or food prior to the service, as well as providing a useful loo stop.

There were also guests attending the funeral from afar who stayed overnight at the Inn, and often we hosted close family to dine in our restaurant on the night of the funeral. All these arrangements needed to be handled sensitively and thoroughly to gain the organiser's confidence and ensure it met with their expectation and accommodated their particular requests. Normally, we managed up to sixty guests but on one or two occasions this swelled to more than 100 and on one particular occasion to well over 150. This was the funeral tea for Dave Skinner, our very dear friend and regular supporter of the Inn. Fortunately, the day of Dave's service was lovely and sunny and the funeral tea was as much outside on the street and in the churchyard as it was in the restaurant and bar. Following a very moving service in the packed church, the funeral tea was an extended celebration of Dave's life, with mini-cones of fish and chips and dinky steak pies from Dales butchers next door, being served up, along with cream cakes and all sorts of other nibbles. Champagne, gin and tonics and beer were flowing like the River Lune and I had no doubt that Dave was looking down and enjoying watching everyone celebrating his life. He just loved watching others enjoy themselves in life and I am sure he would have done so in death.

It was a joy to our family that I was able to host my dad's funeral tea at the Inn. It felt just right somehow and we gave him a joyous send-off with a lovely church service next door, featuring loud organ music, readings, poems and kind words. But what made it even more special was hearing St Mary's bells - first solemnly accompanying Dad into the church, as we pallbearers bore him high upon our shoulders in his oak coffin, and afterwards as we left, chiming with a respectful, dignified and joyous tone. The bells seemed to define the passing of an age and allowed me at the same time to pass a tear of joy and sadness to his life.

There were certain sections of the churchyard which felt a little like my own backyard, where I mowed the grass during the summer months. I was pleased to carry out this modest charitable duty as I always felt it important to give something back to the community. I'd cheekily gently nudge one or two of the gravestones with the mower and silently ask the resident if they would put in a good word for me 'up there' when my own time came. On other days though, when the sun would be shining over the Lune valley and things were going well, it often occurred to me that heaven was right here and now, not in some obscure life after death. Such was the magic of this special Kirkby Lonsdale life we had been privileged to be a part of. It reminded me to make the most of and enjoy every single day. As the saying goes: 'You are a long time dead.'

# Suppliers

Lucy's approach to sales was similarly applied to buying. 'All things being equal, people buy from people they like and trust.'

This is also true when things are not so equal and the price or the product not so favourable. They still buy from people they like and trust.

Our longest-serving suppliers were those who had gone out of their way to get to know us and found ways to add value to our business. These suppliers were often dealing in goods that others could supply, some possibly even cheaper; but the overriding factor was that we trusted them as they had our customers' and our business's best interest in mind when supplying us.

A case in point was our wine supplier EWGA (European Wine growers Association). Jeanette was our contact right from six weeks before opening through until we sold the business. We met her following two visits to other wine suppliers. The others were pleasant, allowing us to try a range of wines to include on our wine list, all very helpful. But it was Jeanette who wanted to know in detail the sort of operation we intended to run, the types of customers we wanted to attract, the space we had for wine storage and how many deliveries we might need each week, and so on. She helped us develop a strategy for selling wine and creating a comprehensive wine list that had a wide range of grape varieties from different wine-growing regions and countries and away from the high-street brands presented at supermarkets.

All this was backed up with assistance in training us and our staff not just how to describe the various wines but also to create a story around a number of them to stimulate customers' interest and encourage them to buy. Before we opened, Jeanette presented a number of attractive clear Perspex ice-buckets that instantly caught the attention, together with bottle openers and menu covers.

Helping to set out our stall like this was so invaluable at this frantic early stage and it continued throughout our eleven years of ownership with two reviews each year of our wine sales and margins as well as an annual invite to a most extensive wine-tasting day. Jeanette's account management continued to help us grow our wine sales year on year, and after a few years we introduced three or four annual dinners and wine tastings which we called Posh Noshers. At these, Jeanette or a wine representative would give a talk on each wine that we paired with a food course. The evenings were well attended and often ensured that our bedrooms and restaurant were filled on what might otherwise be a quiet Monday evening in the depths of winter. Jeanette also further helped us to develop the selection of wine glasses we used from a supplier called Riedal. Their range of wine glasses were designed to allow each different wine to flow over different parts of your tongue as you drank. From a Chardonnay to a Viognier or a Burgundy and on to a Rioja, they had a glass to match; it's amazing what a difference that makes. You can get a rough idea at home by seeing how different a nice red wine tastes out of a large bulbous red-wine glass compared with a small white-wine glass. These glasses add about another ten to fifteen per cent value to the quality of the wine.

Ultimately, it was not just the quality of the product itself that Jeanette was selling but her experience and skill in helping us to add that extra value, creating an experience for the customer which in turn helped to grow sales. You can see how we came to both trust and like her. Many other wine suppliers would come touting for the business but none could break that very strong 'trust-and-like' bond that had been built up.

I don't want you to get a false impression that everything was always perfect. As with any supplier, there were occasional challenges on deliveries and prices but each one was met with honesty and a positive desire to resolve. Like our accountants Moore and Smalley, EWGA and many others were models of what a great supplier should be. They turn a commodity into a high-value product.

We adopted a clear principle about always using local suppliers, not because it was trendy and we could stick it all over our restaurant walls as many brands do these days, but because our success was inextricably linked to Kirkby Lonsdale's success. Visitors coming to stay with us were charmed by the number of independent high-quality stores, traditional butchers, bakers, ironmongers, perfumiers, chocolatiers, sweetshops, ladies' fashion outlets, and so on. These businesses needed our residents to spend in their shops and we needed them to continue trading successfully to provide the attraction for guests staying with us in the first place. One particularly shop stands out as being very successful in attracting our customers to spend in their business, Bijou Blue, which was opened by Rachel and Helen about three years into us running the Inn. Bijou Blue was right across the road from the Sun Inn, guests in room three had an excellent preview into the shop and had often identified their purchases before stepping foot inside. But Rachel and Helen brought further excitement to the guests of the inn by displaying three fluorescent mannequins in their shop window, each modeling an outfit of the exquisite lingerie with which they launched their business.

Only rarely would a shop be vacant in Kirkby Lonsdale for more than a couple of weeks, unlike many market towns around the country. It also had the added benefit that if we traded with the local suppliers then they would likely use our bar and restaurant in return, which they did!

We always felt it important for our residents to have a healthy number of locals in our bar. They added value with their cheerful banter and their sociable relaxed style. Our residents from further afield would often feel they were entering a piece of England that you only found in films. They just loved the rich heritage of locals, a mix of truly local families and many others who had moved to Kirkby Lonsdale themselves because of the friendly welcome and conviviality, all happy to share the good mood of the bar residents.

The Bath House products we used in the bedroom such as soaps, body-washes, perfumes and creams, inspired our guests to visit the Bath House shop in the town. The bacon or sausages for breakfast would always prompt the question, 'Where do you get *these* from?', later that day, we'd often have a load of meat stored in the fridge for a guest who visited Dales butchers next door or cheese from Churchmouse Cheeses. This same story would occur with a range of products including our world-famous pillow-top mattress beds made by Sealy in North Cumbria.

You see, we wanted our guests not only to receive great hospitality and service but also to experience the flavour of the great products and skills the people this region had to offer, and to be inspired by products they could not find at home or on their high street. Such was the magic of Kirkby Lonsdale, the Lune Valley and Cumbria at large.

One aspect regarding some suppliers which always grated was when a representative turned up without an appointment and expected us or a member of the team to drop what they were doing and spend fifteen to twenty minutes discussing their product range or some supply arrangements. Even a five-to-ten minute chat could put you behind if you were running a shift, as in our business we were always up against the deadlines of breakfast, lunch or dinner. If we were not preparing for service to begin, the *mise-en-place*, we were actually serving customers. So even if you showed courtesy, at the back of your mind you were thinking about what yet had to be done, and you could not give your undivided attention. It was challenging enough to stop-start for customers during these periods without the added strain of suppliers. The good account managers always made an appointment in advance so we could plan to give them our undivided attention.

This approach applied equally to local trades. At first, we were in the hands of our project manager using trades from afar, until we had the time and confidence to project-manage ourselves. We were particularly lucky to be introduced by Ty and Janet Power, two of our regular customers to Keith Pryce, a local builder.

In the early days Ty and Janet like so many locals, gave us loads of moral support, and we have some very fond memories of them. One particularly stands out when Ty and Janet assisted us in breaking into our own premises! They were strolling by late at night and we had returned from a rare evening out to find that Tom, our then Supervisor, had locked up the Inn and gone home. Fortunately, Ty and Janet's son Phil was with them and, being much younger and more athletic than us, he climbed the scaffolding (we were in the middle of roof repairs) to gain entry. Such kindness and assistance is what living in Kirkby is all about.

Anyway, our introduction to Keith Pryce made a tremendous difference and gave us the confidence to crack on developing the product. Keith is such a lovely man, very caring and understanding of the challenges a 400-year-old Grade 2 listed building presented. If there was a building crisis, Keith was there in a flash, shoring us up and returning later to resolve the challenge. And when he was helping us on major projects, such as the new kitchen and toilets, you just knew you were in good hands.

Whether for major works or minor, we kept to the same trades people for continuity. Martin, another son of Ty & Janet, was our plumber. Actually, he was more than just a plumber. For perhaps seventy per cent of the year he really was a plumber, but for the remainder he worked as a bookie and had pitches at some of the major racecourses in the UK. His bulging muscles and charming personality brought a smile and often a giggle to many of the female members of the team every time he visited.

Darren our decorator came every Monday while the Inn was closed to carry out small maintenance jobs and any touching-up of paintwork. He is a cheeky chappie, very observant, full of emotional intelligence, who always lifted the mood with the team. Park and Whitely were our electricians and, of course, our resident cabinet-maker was Lucy's dad Tony.

It was Tony who transformed the building in looks and style from a Pub to a five star Inn. I have already talked about the cabinet work Tony made for us prior to purchasing the Inn, but it was his work over the 11 years that added that five star je ne sais quoi.

Tony was prolific with his work. Aged between 71 and 80 he made all the panneling in the bar, the fireplace, the front door and 4 others, the bar top, the wine and cheese cabinets, the tables in the restaurant and many in the bar. The desks, bedheads, side tables, coffee tables and magazine racks in all eleven bedrooms and of course the charmed 'ear plug' boxes too, along with many other bits and peices. All this was made in his garage in Morecambe and transported in his little Toyoto Yaris car. It's fair to say that he was our most treasured supplier, most precious Father and a Father in law that I had the utmost respect for. We have a number of his treasured doors and pieces of furniture in our house today and everytime I paint, polish or move a piece of his work I feel the love that he put into wood and our lives. His sad passing has elevated his work, in our minds, into mythical proportions, which is justly deserved for an outstanding craftsman.

The challenge for all these trades was the age of the building and the way it had been changed, upgraded and adapted over the years. This often meant one job could create another, such was the charm of this seventeenth-century building. Fortunately, all these guys were patient and understanding, both with the building and me. However, on more than one occasion we had to try and cover up from our guests the expletives from the cabinet-maker, such was his usual war cry: 'Is there nothing ******* square in this building?'

Prompt payment for goods was in our DNA. We trusted the suppliers to deliver great products on time, and in return we did the same with our payments. Trust and reputation with the local suppliers were an important dynamic for the good standing of the business. Late payment would suggest that all was not well with an enterprise and your reputation could be put in doubt. Kirkby is a small town and word quickly gets out. We normally had two payment runs each month, and it was also in our interests to keep on top of outstanding invoices so we could easily prepare a cash-flow document and an accurate profit and loss account each month.

Cash flow was an area that we generally kept under control by paying invoices promptly, not over-spending and forecasting cash flows in advance. We did however get into trouble when we invested a large amount of capital for the kitchen and bedrooms. For calculating our return on capital, we removed VAT from the costs of the works and inadvertently used these same figures for our cash-flow projections, forgetting to add the VAT that we would claim back later. We knew we were very close to the wire with our capital spends so we were watching cash-flow projections carefully each week. Unfortunately our projections were not matching our actual spends and alarm bells were sounding much louder than the bells next door. We had forgotten to include the VAT in our project costs.

It's times like this that a business can be brought down. It would have been difficult and expensive to go back to the bank for a larger loan. The economic climate was not good; it was during the credit crunch and we were over exposed by about £30K. We believed we could find this amount over the next six months of trading, but we needed the money now.

Fortunately, at the time government stepped in to help businesses allowing them to delay paying VAT along with other measures to keep the economy going. We were trading well but we had just overspent. So we gave the hardship line to the revenue office, explained that we could pay the VAT due by a certain date a few months later in the year, and they went with it. Normally VAT is the first thing to pay when you are in trouble, as they normally pull the plug first and enforce receivership.

We were very lucky. It was a very sobering experience. All that effort and energy we had put in could have forced us into severe financial trouble.

Relationships with delivery people were also worth investing in. Steve our manager would always give the dray men a cup of coffee; Sam our chef would always have a kind, if fleeting, word for the time-strapped driver, and Natalia in housekeeping would always know from the driver what was going on back at the laundry. These people could make life much easier for you. An offer of a cup of tea/coffee to a tradesman doing a job in the building could make a substantial difference to the mood, speed and ease in which the job was carried out. It was like oiling the wheels. Often one kindness results in another returned, just like Newton's Law: For every action there is an equal and opposite reaction.

It's not just suppliers that helped us build our unique offer but it was also loyal customers. Living close by was a renowned saxophonist who was and still is as I write this book a member of Supertramp. John on one or two rare occasions would strike up at the inn and play to the absolute joy of all present. He was very generous with his time and energy, contributing a great deal to the school and many things locally. Along with one of his sound engineers he helped us to design a very good sound system for the bar and created a range of jazz playlists including another of his bands 'Crème Anglaise' whose CDs we sold to customers who had a following for his great sound.

One manager I worked with believed that this hospitality business is built on love. Love your customers, love your staff and love your suppliers. It's a funny sort of instinctive, intangible feel that you get when you walk into a bar, restaurant or hotel. You definitely know as a customer if the vibe is good or not, if the place is loved and you can feel warmth and care in the air. One bad link in the complex chain of interactions can often have a knock-on effect around the whole building. We saw suppliers as a big link in that chain and were always mindful of the important contribution they made towards the success of our business.

Having such great suppliers on our door step certainly helped make the Sun Inn special for our guests and often made life a whole lot easier for our staff.

# 22

# Parking and Competition

The Sun Inn was designed and built in the era of the horse and carriage, when I believe the London to Scotland stagecoach ran through Kirkby Lonsdale, taking between ten to fourteen days in the 1700s, to reach its final destination. So, passengers would have no doubt stayed at the Sun Inn and many other local hostelries. It is said that the town crier would read out the news from under the overhang section at the front of the building. In those days a stream flowed by the entrance; it now runs through a covered drain.

More recently, I've seen pictures from the 1960s with cars parked one behind another in Church Walk at the side of the Inn. At some point after this, the road was made into a pedestrian walkway and a barrier installed to stop cars entering. You can understand this as at the end of the walkway is a set of ornate and imposing gates built in the 1800s. The gates are eye-catching and have an ingenious mechanism to ensure they always return to their closed position when anyone passes through. They lead to the churchyard and St Mary's Church with its Norman tower and flying buttresses and, beyond to Ruskin's View with the idyllic scene of the River Lune and the pasture and fells beyond. Part of the charm of the Inn is this setting - a vignette of England's landscape at its best.

This is all well and good, but the busy narrow one-way Market Street with its double-yellow lines is a challenge for today's guests, who often turn up with large cars and big expectations to match. You can imagine the logistical issues that arise in such a narrow road when they pull up outside the front of the Inn to drop off their luggage and check in!

We purchased the Inn knowing this, but safe in the knowledge that for the last number of years customers had accepted the parking challenge, and at that time free parking was readily available at the other side of the church on Queen's Square and further up the road at Fairbank, (this meant parking beyond the old blacksmith's forge where well-known Kirkby character Jonty Wilson carried out his trade before becoming a writer and broadcaster about Kirkby Lonsdale life). In those early months after acquiring the Inn, we only had between five and eight letting rooms and a occupancy around sixty per cent so the parking challenge could be measured as a mere irritation or inconvenience by our customers. However, by the time we had eleven rooms and occupancy was in the nineties per cent during the summer months, the drop-off point challenge rose to complaint level for customers, pedestrians and local motorists. The only way this was heading was a clampdown by the authorities, which would have put our most valuable source of revenue, namely accommodation, in jeopardy.

By now we had generally established ourselves in the town as a quality establishment and a force for good. We had a business that was attracting new visitors who spent money in the shops, and we were spending money with local suppliers to service our clients, while also providing another attractive facility for the locals to frequent. All in all, our business success was generally well received and supported.

For a number of years, Alan Day chaired Kirkby Lonsdale Town Council. A dapper, diminutive man with a tough constitution, Alan is noted for always sporting highly polished shoes, possibly a hand-on from his early naval career. This was followed by a life working in retail, from which I'm sure he shared our entrepreneurial spirit. He is a stickler for standards and loves seeing the town vibrant, neat, tidy and attractive. He can often be seen walking around and stopping for a coffee or a chat with locals and visitors. And he takes great pleasure in seeing traders washing down shop fronts, assembling window displays, tending hanging baskets, and presenting their goods with flair and imagination. I'm sure as town council chairman he came in for some flak on occasion, but his head and heart have always been with the prosperity and sustainability of the town and its people.

I remember discussing the challenge of parking for our business in those early years, and he was kind enough to arrange for the barrier at the entrance of Church Walk to be moved back five or six metres to allow for a car to pull off the road. This wasn't just for the Sun Inn's benefit: the cheese shop next door and the houses on Church Walk also saw an improvement, particularly as cars had been previously pulling up on the pavement. This newly-formed drop-off point eliminated the blockages on the road and all the chaos they caused.

It was a game-changer for us. We could now brief residents at the reservation stage to pull in beside the Inn, so that they could unload their luggage without some other motorist beeping his horn in frustration and the flow of traffic grinding to a halt. The guests could then be shown the public car park they were able to use for the duration of their stay.

It was one of those practical arrangements that eliminated all the challenges, and took the sting out of that key 'first impressions' moment when guests arrive. Thanks to Alan's help, we were able to improve the prosperity of both our own business and that of other town enterprises with whom we traded. By that time, TripAdvisor was starting to become a key influence on customers about where to stay and it was with relief that unfavourable comments on parking were for now considerably reduced.

Solving this issue helped to ensure all was going well for the Sun Inn; until, that is, our success was challenged. When we launched our business, we were the 'new kids on the block', clearly new competition for the pubs and restaurants in the town. But it wasn't too long before we, too, found ourselves being challenged. This followed the opening of two new prestigious establishments in Kirkby Lonsdale. First was Plato's with eight rooms, and this was quickly followed by the Royal with fourteen. At the same time we saw an increase in other competition with a variety of apartments, cottages and houses being given over to tourist accommodation. It seemed our prosperity, perhaps even our livelihood, might be under threat.

Interestingly, as part of the conditions imposed by our bank, we had to have our business valued in August 2007, which was prior to the reopening of the Royal Hotel. This comprehensive valuation turned out as we had expected; but the possibility of the Royal re-opening actually had a detrimental effect on the valuation. It was assumed that we would not be able to maintain the same levels of trade and profit once there was new competition in town and down went our valuation. So it was actually in our interests for the Royal Hotel to be up and running so we could demonstrate that we were able to hold our share of the market and maintain profit levels which would boost the value of our business almost overnight.

Previously, while working for corporate companies in Plymouth and Chester, I'd experienced the threat caused by 'new supply' entering the market. The implications were on a much larger scale than for our business in Kirkby Lonsdale and the experience prepared me for the effect our new competition might well have on sales. It also meant I could work out how to manage our way through the challenge. In some ways, I could see a distinct advantage competition might bring. Firstly, residents staying in the new competition for two or three days are likely to eat out at least once or twice and we could hopefully secure more diners. If we were able to charm and delight these customers better than the competition, the next time they visited Kirkby Lonsdale they might choose to stay with us. Secondly, these two new properties would help raise the profile of the town as a honeypot tourist destination and help drive new customers for us all to prosper by.

What Lucy and I had not considered were the effects of the new competition on parking provision in the town. We'd managed to head off any impact on sales; in fact, we grew slightly. However, the rate of growth in the first year certainly diminished with the advent of this new competition.

Although sales growth was soon back to normal a year or two later as overall growth in accommodation in Kirkby Lonsdale increased to fill supply, there was inevitably an impact on parking. Those places where residents could park for free were increasingly taken up with more hospitality customers and rising numbers of staff who travelled to the town in cars to service them. Staff who could not afford the cost of public car parks were parking in residential areas of the town; taking up residential spaces and blocking entrances, and impeding access to certain roads for emergency vehicles. Parking had become a serious issue for both the townspeople and ourselves and the issue began once again to appear on our TripAdvisor reviews, as well as complaints made directly to us.

We had been invited to attend a workshop that the then new chairman of the town council, Allan Muirhead, set up to encourage residents and shopkeepers to help shape the future of the town. A number of issues arose, including broadband, housing, the weekly market. But, for me, the most pressing problem was the parking challenge. Because of this, and the fact I felt it time to put something back into the community, I volunteered to chair the parking group.

For anyone who gets involved in parking it comes with a serious health warning. The subject is highly emotive, arousing intense feelings. Everyone seems to have a view on the subject and they vary dramatically from each individual standpoint. Often such views are delivered with only half the picture in mind. They would go something like this:

'It's ridiculous; we need more parking in the town.'

'We don't want more parking; the town is already overrun with cars and people as it is.'

'The public car parks charge too much and everyone keeps going round and round to find free parking.'

'Parking by the school is ridiculous; something needs to be done before a child has an accident or, worse still, is killed.'

'Customers don't stay long in the shops, bars and restaurants. They have to get back to their cars before the ticket runs out.'

'The traffic wardens are far too zealous; they're putting customers off visiting the town.'

'It's SLDC's fault.'

'It's the school's fault.'

And so on – a whole cocktail of frustration and strongly held beliefs. We started with a discussion document and looked for support to consider the question holistically. We eventually set up a group that represented town and district council, schools, traders, residents, emergency services and politicians from every side. But getting everyone onside and around a table was a challenge to say the least and this took over a year. Even then it was compromised. The next year was spent on research.

A wonderful group of town volunteers recorded the numbers of cars parked in the town on streets, car parks and alleyways, by time of day, day of the week and time of the year. A most amazing amount of data, that gave great insight. In addition, we carried out a comprehensive opinion survey in conjunction with the South Lakeland District Council (SLDC) research department, gaining around 400 views and opinions for the town of approximately 2,000 residents. We also held a drop-in day for locals and traders to express their views on a number of parking topics. All this information was professionally analysed and then considered by the group from which a number of initiatives were formed to shape and build a long-term resolution to the challenges; all this was endorsed by a public meeting in the town.

To our dismay, over the next two years the implementation of many of these initiatives was strung out, delayed, blocked or ignored by departments of SLDC and others. This was, in my view, due to the lucrative funding that parking provided for the council without the balance and due consideration to the needs and wishes of the local community.

Our voice could be heard, persistently, but was all too often ignored. It was like running water uphill or being stuck in treacle. We did have a couple of small wins and were able to promote some cost-effective car-permit arrangements for the accommodation providers to direct their guests off the streets and into the car parks. I have to say this did help the Sun Inn and Plato's considerably and slightly opened up free parking spaces in the town. What also helped were some arrangements for the better safety of schoolchildren, the reduced price of short-stay public car parking and new car park signage. But the fundamental changes in the arrangements and approach to build in parking solutions were not to be delivered. There was only a certain level of commitment and staying power a group like this could sustain. After more than four years and two chairpersons, the group disbanded. The hours of research work by the volunteers, the number of group meetings and discussions with officials had all been in vain.

A great deal of thanks needs to be given to all those who gave up their valuable time and so valiantly fought the mission to improve parking in Kirkby Lonsdale. We can at least say we gave it our best shot and for anyone who takes on this subject we can at least demonstrate the health warnings that come with this very vexed subject of parking and the entrenched position held by the district council.

# Selling up

In our first year of trading, I was fifty years old; a decade later the sixtieth birthday milestone triggered a need to review my life. If all goes well, I thought, I may have just completed two-thirds of my allotted life span. Of course, there is no guarantee as to how long a person will live, but it was clear that my physically strongest years were behind me. However, with luck, I may begin to gently mature – like a fine wine before it goes past its best.

Due to the size of the business and the hands-on approach we adopted in its running, our roles were physically demanding. Within the next five years we should either have had to employ a person to run our entire business and step right out to let them run the Sun Inn without constant interference, or sell up.

It was clear that to keep going would test energy levels to destruction and have a detrimental effect on my physical and mental health, not to mention the likely impact on the business.

Lucy and I had to be really honest with ourselves and ask if we could let go. It had been our baby for such a long time and the business had grown into something quite substantial and our good fortune was wrapped up in it. Also, the relationship with our customers and staff was so very personal. Could we really hand all this over? Could we truly delegate authority and responsibility to another person without selling it lock stock and barrel? I think perhaps Lucy could have seen us managing from a distance to give that person the space and authority, but I was uncertain as to whether I could trust myself not to interfere and over manage.

Throughout my life, I've never looked back, only forward. Sure, I have learnt from my mistakes and have some wonderful memories to cherish, but I have never dwelt on the past. I have never felt hard done by, I can't say why, except that I've always taken the approach: it's not what you've got or where you're at that counts, however painful and for whatever reason at the time, what counts far more is what you make of what you've got. This approach has driven me on; helped me battle against the odds, never giving up, never surrendering. It has been engraved into my very being. This constant striving seemed to define my existence and to now arrive at the point where I'd give in to an easier, more comfortable life seemed all unsettling.

We always had a ten-year vision. When customers and staff asked about our plans, we were always very open and said we would review the situation after ten years to see if we still had the same stamina, will and enthusiasm to carry on further. Now after my sixtieth birthday, Lucy and I felt this time had come. Plans were already in place to allow it to happen, should we make that decision. Our accountants, Moore and Smalley, had been working with us for the past three years with projections and calculations for our exit strategy. We had had the business valued by Christie & Co and the valuation had come out at the top end of our expectation. Yet we hesitated. What was it that was stopping us from getting out?

The truth of the matter is that we were scared to go through the process: there was so much at risk, things that could go wrong, and so much to lose. It seemed like our whole being was wrapped up in The Sun Inn, it almost defined us; our business struggles and challenges were such a part of our lives, what we hung on to and fought for so strongly.

The first of our worries was about the staff. A change of ownership could create a whole new set of dynamics for the team. Would they get on with new owners? Would they have to prove themselves all over again? Would they feel at risk, especially those with commitments like mortgages and kids? Would they feel we'd let them down? Would key members of staff leave and weaken the team while we were trying to sell?

Secondly, when customers get wind of the business being up for sale, would it affect sales and profits? If it took two or three years to sell, the business might be substantially devalued as guests took flight, which our retirement projections did not allow for. The business had never gone backwards and we might come to feel we were caught in a trap.

A valuation is only a valuation. A sale is only a sale when the money is in the bank. What was the likelihood of getting the valuation price?

More questions. Who should we get to sell it? Should we do it ourselves? Should we get an agent? Should we try to sell it discreetly, informing the staff and relying on them to keep quiet so customers were unaware until a sale was secured?

If we sold and got the money we needed, we'd have to invest it. This wouldn't come without risk, especially in investments such as stocks and shares, where we had little experience.

We were not just selling bricks and mortar like a house, but a living, complex business. This would come with much paperwork, needing assurances and undertakings all protected by law that could be tricky to navigate. We would have to find a good solicitor experienced in these matters to help us through.

There were ever more questions. How expensive would all this be? How much money would be taken in tax?

These were all the questions that swirled around our heads in addition to handling the day-to-day business. We found it all quite overwhelming and easier to put off than tackle.

For my sixtieth birthday, I had arranged to take Lucy and my kids on a sailing holiday to Greece. It was the first time for many years that I was in a position to do this. We chartered a very swish sailboat with a skipper and a cook and sailed away with fresh wind and sunshine in our hair. To be so close to my kids, physically and emotionally, and to establish a close bond with my new daughter-in-law Lori Ann was simply wonderful. I realised all that had been missing in my busy life.

My kids had grown up. Much of their first ten years I'd been apart from them because of the sad divorce, and much of the last ten years we'd always been working at the Inn. They were all very good and would often visit or I would escape and see them for a couple of days. But it was now, with the sale of the Inn, that I would have the opportunity to try to reverse things a little. Time to simply watch, support and marvel at the joy they bring me, just by their being themselves now they had turned from children to adults. I realised how very proud I was of them, not for what they were doing but because of what they were as people, their values, their outlook on life and the energy they put into their endeavours. Many of these traits were nurtured by their Mum, and I can take little credit. I am so very grateful to her for all the dedication, love and support given as they grew from babies to adults. The result is so impressive.

Gemma was by now Resident Choreographer for *Matilda* at the Cambridge Theatre in London's West End. My eldest boy Austin had become a notational analyst working with the national England football teams. Kirsty, who originally trained as a nutritionist, switched to dance, retrained and was now working in the show *42nd Street* again in the West End. And my youngest was now a world professional squash player. Where had the time gone when they were children? Time stops for no man, and Austin and Lori Ann wasted none in producing the next generation of the family, my first grandson Jacob. Timing suggests it may have been that motion in the ocean that was the contributing factor, so for a number of reasons that holiday had a transformational effect on the Fuller lives.

What this time away with them made me realise was just how much I had missed with them, watching and admiring how they handle all the challenges that face adults as they make their way through life. It seemed such a compelling reason to seize the moment and take the plunge, sell the Inn and start a new life.

During that holiday, Lucy and I celebrated our eleventh wedding anniversary, so we decided to mark the date by giving each other and our marriage an appraisal. It was done slightly in jest but was nevertheless a useful exercise. We made notes for a day or two in advance and on a bright sunny morning sitting up in bed overlooking the Greek islands with a cup of tea in hand, we carefully submitted our thoughts. I'm sure you can guess who came out of it best, and it wasn't me! We were both, however, guilty of giving our lives to the Inn and not enough to each other. In fact, we concluded it was pretty amazing that we'd survived as a married couple at all, such were the relentless stresses and strains of the hospitality business that continuously imposed itself on our private lives.

It was then that we both finally concluded that it was time to take that brave step to sell the Inn. Actually, Lucy had been ready to do this for a while, but we'd gone in together and we were going out together. The big prizes were to find each other again; not that we had lost each other exactly, but our marriage was too crowded and tied up with the business and we needed it cleansed, refreshed and returned to what it was like when we were first married. Together with time to spend time with my children and grandchildren.

These prizes, this opportunity, now became our mission. We locked onto the target and started to get preparations underway, striking while the iron was hot.

Our first port of call was with our trusted accountants to make sure we really understood the numbers: how the tax might be apportioned, budgeting the costs of sale, forecasting best- and worst-case scenarios and outcomes to finally check we were really happy to push the button.

Colin was particularly helpful advising on solicitors we might approach with whom he had worked with on past sales. This was a great starting point in our selection process, and so very useful to have his experience of the challenges that go with such a sale.

We considered local and regional agents, but in the end concluded we needed regional and national coverage to ensure sufficient interest for both a timely sale and one at the right price. What we might pay extra in agent's fees could be outweighed by gaining greater interest and a good sale price. We interviewed two of the top agents in this field, Christie & Co and Colliers.

Christie & Co were obviously front runners because they had already valued the Inn twice before and had a good handle on the business's true worth; but what really sold them to us was the personal touch offered by their representative Keith. You will recall the 'Trust and Like' dimension that I've already mentioned for both sellers and buyers, well Christie & Co's Keith won us over on this. You see, it's not just about finding a buyer, it's about getting the buyer across the finishing line within tight deadlines, and this is not always easy. It needs a good agent to overcome the log jams between competing solicitors to get the best deal out of the contract; the banks to provide the loans and accountants to set up trading companies, and so on. So often buyers can falter at the last minute over funding or contractual complications, and sellers get impatient over the time it's taking. Either can withdraw from the market for various reasons, including the adverse effects a sale is having on the business. Perhaps the vendor decides to put it back on the market to try for a different buyer, or the buyer gets impatient and withdraws an offer. To keep all these various parties onside and moving swiftly towards completion can often take skill and diplomacy from a third party and Keith was that important extra dimension in getting us across the line.

Keith worked with us closely to craft the particulars, pulling out the key selling messages and compelling reasons to justify the price tag on offer. We set a fair price based on the valuation with a view to just minimal discount if we had to. We were not going to barter a high price tag and heavy discount. Our view was to attract the interest we needed to set a value-for-money price and be confident in any negotiation.

While all this was going on, we gathered the top team members of the Inn together and broke the news. We'd always been open and honest with the team and in this departing period it was to be no different. Before we released the selling details to the market, we wanted to share our thoughts and prepare them for the uncertainties ahead so we could involve them in each of the steps we were about to take. As you can imagine, this was relayed and received with much emotion: tears, understanding, kind words and a sort of togetherness that you want to hang on to, but you know is going to slip away all too soon.

We prepared ourselves and the team for a long-drawn-out sale. We had witnessed properties on the market for a long time, up to three years and more. Our approach was to continue to invest in the property and run it exactly as we had done for the past ten years while we were seeking a buyer. It was greatly in our interests to demonstrate a well kept and lively product. If our enthusiasm wavered, we were sure this would rub off on the staff. Three years was a long time but, in a way, it helped to soften the blow to the staff. We were also clear to explain that even if we attracted a buyer tomorrow it could take four to six months to transact a sale. Our promise was to keep our employees updated at each stage, protect them with legislation know as T.U.P.E (Transfer of Undertakings (Protection of Employment) Regulations) We would work with them over the coming months to cement the skill base they had, to ensure they had full confidence in their current roles and make them completely aware of all their rights and entitlements. We would keep the entire staff informed at every stage, from the property going on the market and through each key development of the sale.

Of course, we knew that once we told the staff, the news would be quickly out around town and the intrigue begin; but this settled down after the initial flurry and the staff seemed relaxed with our honest and open approach. We had navigated the first hurdle by September 2016.

That October, we had two viewings lined up, both from couples; one with and one without hotel/catering experience. One of the names was familiar to me, Iain and Jenny Black. It would be a real turn-up for the book if it was the same Iain I worked with while still at school, cooking burgers over charcoal at a place called the Canadian Charcoal Pit in Hale, Cheshire, and then later when our paths crossed working for Forte hotels as general managers. As luck would have it, it was this Iain who walked through the door for a viewing. He was still in corporate life at a hotel in Manchester and keen to escape; just as I had been all those years earlier.

There was an immediate synergy and, after a couple of viewings and subsequent overnight stay, the offer was made. The rest, as they say, is history. Fate had secured a timely sale to an owner-operator. The townspeople would be happy, and we sure were; Lucy and I were delighted to have achieved our objective; but, perhaps most importantly, Iain and Jenny were pleased to embark on a very different life away from the corporate world.

For the last eleven years, Lucy and I had never felt we fully owned the Inn rather that we were merely custodians of a very special property. Since the 1600s, hospitality, food and drink had been traded by generations of owners and innkeepers. We felt it our job to leave this historic building in a better state than we found it and fit to service the needs and wants of today's customers. We left the building on 8th May, 2017, with so very many happy memories, having secured a sale price that reflected the growth and development of the business and the hard work and dedication we'd put in, and in the safe knowledge that the Inn was now in the next pair of safe hands to continue its history, run by dedicated people in their own way in their own style, just as we had endeavoured to do. There were no regrets; the time was right, the prize was a new way of life for Lucy and me to enjoy.

Writing this book has been the first time that I have looked back and examined my life. I feel very privileged to have had such a smashing partner to have shared this big hairy audacious experience with, and I know that without the very special people of Kirkby Lonsdale and our family, friends, mentors, staff and parents, none of this would have been possible. Lucy and I thank them all from the bottom of our hearts, especially those who have not been mentioned by name in the book, but who nevertheless contributed in making the Inn so special through their hard work and dedication.

As Frank Herbert said: *There is no real ending. It's just the place where you stop the story.*

Well the story has ended but our lives have not and I remain extremely excited to discover what this next chapter, in the final third of my life, may bring.

Thank you for taking the time to read our adventure and do hope it struck a chord with your adventure in life too.

# Return on Capital Investment (the detail)

This final chapter is designed for those who want to gain detailed insight in our approach to the return on capital investment, a vital aspect of the business. This understanding is what brought our financial success.

I have fitted it in at the end of the book so as not to interrupt the flow of the story. This is my simple take on how the return on capital investment relates to a freehold hotel business. If you are interested in more of the detail, read on.

Accountants and valuers add lots of complicated indices, formulae, fancy jargon and varying methods. But I will explain my understanding of the subject and how we applied it.

## Valuation

As a starting point, I want to cover how pubs, inns and hotels are generally valued; to do this you need to refer to a profit and loss account, so I have included a typical example showing all the sales and costs of a small inn, in Appendix 1

Freehold hotels, inns and pubs are broadly valued on either a set multiple of the profit returned, assuming the building is in good condition, or on a bricks-and-mortar value, whichever is higher. If, as in our case, the roof needed replacing, adjustments needed to be made against the valuation based on the profit returned.

The industry seeks to make a 10 per cent return on the total capital invested in the building and the business. So if the net book value on the balance sheet or the price you are prepared to pay for the property is £1m, you would expect the business to make a profit each year of £100K. Or vice versa: if the property makes £100K profit you would expect it to be worth around £1m, assuming the building is in good condition, or adjust accordingly. In this first example the annual profit and loss account shows a profit of £118K, which would indicate a business value of around £1.18m. In other words a ten times multiple of EBIT profit.

As we all know, profit is sales less costs; but there are different terms for profit depending on which costs are left in or out, such as gross profit or net profit. The profit terms we are interested in here are EBIT. This is earnings (profit) before the final costs of interest and tax are applied. EBITDA is earnings before the final costs of interest, tax, depreciation and amortisation are applied.

Sometimes the industry value of a freehold business where the building is in good condition is calculated not only around a track record of ten times its annual EBIT profit, but also around seven or eight times its annual EBITDA, shown consistently over a number of years, or valued on a bricks-and-mortar price, whichever is higher.

These multiples can vary slightly. A good property in a stunning lakeside location may command as much as a twelve times multiple of EBIT or a good property in a poor location may be an eight times multiple of EBIT. However, the average is ten.

## Interest/ Borrowings

Interest, as we know, is the cost of borrowing money to help fund all or part of the business. For example, if a bank loans £500K towards purchasing the business at a price of £1m and they ask for an annual interest rate of say 2.5 per cent, it will cost £12.5K of interest each year. However, borrowing sometimes comes from different sources. You may find for instance that £500K was borrowed from the bank and £500K was borrowed from an investor who expected 10 per cent interest (£50K per year) on the loan, or there may be a combination of other shareholders expecting 10 per cent return. In this case, the overall loan would be £1m and the interest cost would be £12.5K + £50.0K = £62.5K each year. Accordingly, the rate of interest on the total loan would be 6.25 per cent. The overall rate of interest is also known as the weighted average cost of capital or the WACC. When making a capital investment, it is important that you know the overall percentage interest on the capital you are borrowing. The WACC quoted here is shown as 6.5 per cent. In some cases, it is simple because you just borrow money from one source, the bank. But where you have multiple loans you have to be clear of the average cost of capital, which is the annual interest cost.

This is because if the business mentioned above makes a 10 per cent EBIT return on capital and the WACC (average interest) is 6.5 per cent, it only leaves 3.5 percent of profit to pay back the £1m debt. In this extreme example of a business being worth £1m, 3.5 per cent profit represents £35K each year. Ignoring the compound factor of interest, if the £1m debt was paid back in one lump sum at the end of the term, all the £35K annual profit would have to be used each year for 28-29 years to pay back the debt, a risky prospect. In most cases, in a commercial situation, the bank want the debt paid back within fifteen years. So you can see the importance of understanding the overall interest rate on your loan and your ability to service the debt over the years and pay back the loan.

## Depreciation

Depreciation also needs to be understood when you calculate return on capital investment. It is the process by which a company allocates an asset's cost over the duration of its useful life. An example is a new washing machine that has a life expectancy of ten years and costs £1,000, which would put a depreciation cost of £100 per year into the profit and loss account for each of the next ten years. A wise owner would hold this cash each year so that he or she could afford to pay for a new machine at the end of ten years and therefore not have to raise further capital. In this respect, we disciplined ourselves to spend each year's total depreciation on replacing capital items and waited towards the end of each year in case of an unexpected necessity to replace other capital items, but planned for items coming to the end of their useful life. In this way you can always keep the boilers, machinery, equipment and fixtures and fittings in good condition by ensuring you have the funds to do so. This allowed us to keep the quality product sustainable and up to date with the latest technology, design or trend for future years. Remember repairs and maintenance spends are there to keep the capital items going for their expected life.

Depreciation and interest are both costs of capital and have to be carefully accounted for when working out the return on capital projects or initiatives that you may be carrying out on the property.

## Types of capital expenditure

There are two types of capital expenditure –defensive and opportunistic. For example, a defensive capital item would be a replacement washing machine which may make no return on capital investment, and replacing the item would generate no additional profit for the business or possibly; say replacing a central heating boiler, which may generate a 2.5 per cent return if it was more efficient than the boiler it replaced. This contrasts with an opportunistic capital spend such as creating a new bedroom which will form a new revenue stream and may make a 30 per cent return on capital investment, through the additional profit it generates for the business.

It's essential that you have a blend of both opportunistic capital expenditure and defensive capital expenditure to get at least an average of 10 per cent return. Otherwise you will reduce the overall return on investment of the business. For example the classic mistake is where somebody buys a business for, say, £1m and it makes £100K at EBIT (the industry average at ten times the EBIT) and then a new owner spends £300K doing it up with new furnishings, fittings and such – all defensive spends and as a result makes gain of £110K EBIT the following year. Here the business is now worth just £1.1m (ten times EBIT); but the owners have now invested £1.3m – and are likely to never get the extra £200K back through this type of capital expenditure.

These may be just words and the concept theoretical, but there's a big difference between refurbishment and redevelopment. Refurbishment is the replacement of furnishings and fittings, just like replacing a new washing machine, curtains, carpets and so on. Whereas redevelopment is the creation of a new product and or service which will appeal to new markets, and create new streams of revenue or increases in revenue through price. It may involve replacement of fixtures and fittings but it targets a specific market opportunity.

When Lucy and I spent capital moving our newly-acquired business from a pub to an inn, it was mainly redevelopment; but there was a proportion of defensive spend as well. Once we purchased the inn, we initially spent £90K: £30K on defensive items such as repairing the roof, and £60K on opportunistic spends, ensuring a blend of the two types of capital investment. The £60K redevelopment money was used to reposition the business in the market place to attract a new clientele. As a result, we were way on track to take the first year's annual profit from £45K EBIT to more than £65K EBIT. We bought the business for £560K and spent an additional £90K to make a total capital investment of £650K. This stabilised the financial business base because when measured using the standard industry multiplier (as 10 x £65K EBIT) it equals £650K capital value. It showed a 10 per cent return on investment. Compare that to our buying the business for £560k when it was showing a 10 x £45K EBIT capital value of £450K. Now you can see both the financial risk and the financial opportunity when we first started out.

You can imagine my relief when the people coming through the door after we closed for redevelopment for the first three weeks, got the fact that it was a new value added product and were prepared to pay slightly more for the goods and services as it had a greater value to them, together with having greater appeal to attract more customers looking for quality. It was not just a name change from a pub to an inn following a spruce-up.

I now want to take you back to that first example, the profit and loss account from Appendix 1. On the face of it, this business looks in good shape and doing quite well in terms of converting sales to profit. Many business owners would be quite happy. However, when looking at return on capital investment, you have to interrogate the figures more closely and understand the profit made from each of the revenue streams in order to quickly understand how the growth or loss of sales in any one area may affect EBIT and EBITDA profit. This is quite easy, but you will be surprised how few owners and managers take this next important step to gain insight into their business

The second example (Appendix 2) shows the same profit-and-loss account example as the previous one, but this time shows the profit made per revenue stream, that is, food, liquor and rooms. The results show a whole different picture.

Accountants often just give you profit and loss in the format of the first example (Appendix 1), and managers and owners leave it at that. However, in the following example, where I show profit by revenue stream, it shows the food side of the business is making a sizeable loss, the liquor an average profit and the rooms a great profit. Clearly each revenue stream must make a profit or at worst break even if it's an essential part of the business.

This is perhaps an extreme case but is often the reality regarding food. If you think about it, the bar person doesn't have to make the item, just simply pour the drink and hand it over to the customer. For the chef, however, it's more complex. To make a steak pie, he has to roll out the pastry, cook the meat, make the pie, peel potatoes and mash them, and so on. Then the waitress has to go to the kitchen and take the food to the table. So the cost of production for a food sale is so much greater, even though the cost of the raw material is about the same for food as for liquor. In the case of the rooms, the cost of sales is very low. The cost of linen, soaps and so on are allocated to direct expenses which, in this example, we've applied as a percentage of sales. Our experience is that expenses for food and drink and those for rooms work out at very similar percentages – around 14.5 per cent of sales for variable expenses and 5 per cent for direct expenses. It's therefore very easy to extract the overall cost of expenses by revenue stream and it's easy of course to allocate wage costs.

Once you understand the conversion of sales to profit by each revenue stream you can quickly and easily see the effect that an increase or decrease in any area would have on profit. As a consequence it makes working out return on investment so much easier as I shall show later.

Digressing slightly, these profit and loss accounts shown by revenue stream demonstrate just how difficult it is to make much profit out of food, unless you are a branded restaurant serving cheap produce such as pizza and pasta at a high mark-up, or places like Nandos that just serve one line of food and have little or no wastage as there's only one main ingredient, in this case, chicken. These places often have high volume and can slightly reduce labour costs due to scale, and they do make money.

The other type of restaurant that can make money is at the top end, such as Heston Blumenthal's Fat Duck. If you can make a 10 per cent conversion from food sales to EBIT you are doing well. To put this into perspective, a 5 per cent shortfall to the conversion of food sales to profit on £200K food sales would cost £10K of EBIT profit; but more importantly when it comes to valuing the property for sale, this could cost you 10 x £10K EBIT or £100K shortfall in the valuation price. Looking at it like this does grab your attention. It certainly did ours as we always had our eyes on the overall valuation for when we retired.

Just on food, our approach was that you must have an appealing food product but always remember that it's a lot of effort providing food for little financial return. You are better off concentrating time and effort on controlling the food related wages and purchases as these can quickly get out of hand, and a lot less time on trying to grow food sales. Greater financial rewards are made from selling more rooms and drinks which will in turn drive turnover.

I often found it difficult to see the logic in discounting food, such as a 10-per-cent-off deal or 2 for the price of 1 promotion. As you can see, a 10 per cent margin cut would have turned the profit into a loss and would certainly cost you money. Yet you see other establishments often doing this, which always makes me wonder if they have interrogated their profit and loss account by revenue stream. This discounting can also detract from the value proposition you are providing in the first place.

## Disruption costs

There's just one other cost to consider when calculating your return on capital investment for an initiative or project, and that's the cost of disruption. For instance, when you convert an existing letting bedroom without a bathroom to create an en-suite bedroom and it cannot be let for, say, three weeks. You need to calculate how much EBIT profit you are losing during this period and add it to project costs such as building materials and labour. You can now calculate this loss of profit by simply multiplying the sales lost by the EBIDA percentage of the relevant revenue stream, which in this example is Rooms. In this sense time is money. If a project overruns the loss of profit is increased, the cost of the works more expensive and therefore this reduces the return on capital investment. Works should be carried out at the quietest time of the year to reduce disruption costs and be very specific with the contractor about the time available for the works to be completed. Often our building works would be finished on the day the firsts guests were arriving. That morning, carpet would go down, furniture and beds installed, pictures put up and rooms cleaned and serviced by 3pm for the guest arrival. It was as close as that.

So that's the preamble. I think we're now just about ready to see how to work out the return on investment on a simple initiative: to convert an unused laundry room to a guest bedroom.

## Return on a new project or initiative

You will see from the example in Appendix 3 that certain assumptions have been made here to work out potential additional revenue. You definitely need to make sure your assumptions are robust. In this case they assume that because each of the other bedrooms at the Inn are filled every weekend and for at least one night mid-week, this new room will be filled to the same pattern. A fairly reasonable assumption, but I would go one step further and also record the turn-away guests who tried without success to make a reservation whenever you are full, to make absolutely sure demand was there. Laborious, I know, but essential; since this establishes exactly how much demand there may have been. If, say, three guests were turned away each night of the year, there would be an opportunity to build three new rooms. This sort of research to truly measure demand is vital if you want to maximize every opportunity and make transformational profit growth. Remember, you can only spend capital once and you have to eliminate as much risk as possible, and detailed research is key along with careful financial calculation.

Now (in Appendix 3) you can see how easy it is to work out sales to profit by using the EBITDA percentage from your adjusted profit and loss account by revenue stream (shown in Appendix 2). Simply take the additional sales and multiply by the EBITDA percentage (which in this case is 60.5%) to show the cash EBITDA profit.

The depreciation cost is different depending on each item. A bed may last for seven years whereas a desk may last for twelve. In Appendix 3, they have played it safe and gone for ten years, or 10 per cent write-off per year overall.

The cost of interest/borrowing money is taken off the annual profit and the loss of profit due to disruption is added to the building costs at £20K.

Here the new room would bring £5,630 additional profit. Building costs and disruption come in at £20K. It would, therefore, make a very good 28 per cent return on capital, and the capital could be paid off in less than four years. A good result for an opportunistic initiative.

Now, to make transformational increased profits, you need to find a lot of these sorts of opportunistic initiatives which, fortunately, we were able to do at the Sun Inn.

## Causal Track

To easily show the cumulative effects of these initiatives, you can use a 'causal track'. This shows exactly what effects a range of capital investments could make on profits, conversion on sales to profit and return on capital investment, together with the relationship of all these projects to the overall future potential value of the business.

You can see from the simple example of a causal track in Appendix 4 what the effects a number of capital investment initiatives can have to the overall value of the business over the ensuing years. In this example, I have simply added some more projects/initiatives using the same rate of return as the example of the unused laundry room, and shown a projection to 2020 where a blend of opportunistic and defensive capital spend is made.

This example of the causal track shows in 2017 capital investment of £1.18m and the sale value of £1.18m, but by the end of 2020 there's a capital investment of £1.3m and a sale value of £1.46m. In other words a further £120K of capital has been invested and as a result the overall business is now worth £280K more. A handsome result.

It's this understanding of return on capital investment that not only ensures you buy the business at the right price, but also allowed you to clinically assess and exploit the future opportunities as you begin to create and monitor demand for each of the revenue streams.

With this insight and the development opportunities we spotted at the Sun Inn, we saw a bright, exciting and profitable future ahead of us very early on.

# Appendix 1
## Outline Profit and Loss Account

| | | % |
|---|---|---|
| Sales | | |
| Food | 200,000 | |
| Liquor | 200,000 | |
| Rooms | 200,000 | |
| **TOTAL** | **600,000** | |
| Purchases | | |
| Food | 64,000 | 32% |
| Liquor | 70,000 | 35% |
| **TOTAL** | **134,000** | |
| **GROSS PROFIT** | **466,000** | |
| Wages | | |
| Kitchen | 76,000 | 38% |
| Front of House | 98,000 | 24.5% |
| Rooms | 24,000 | 12% |
| **TOTAL** | **198,000** | 35% |
| Direct Expenses | | |
| Linen | | |
| Maintenance | | |
| Stationery | | |
| Marketing | | |
| Etc | | |
| **TOTAL** | 87,000 | 14.5% |
| Overheads | | |
| Electricity | | |
| Gas | | |
| Rates | | |
| Insurance | | |
| Etc | | |
| **TOTAL** | **33,000** | **5.6%** |
| **EBITDA** | **148,000** | 25% |
| Depreciation | 30,000 | |
| **EBIT** | **118,000** | **20%** |

# Appendix 2
# Profit and Loss account shown by revenue stream

| Example P & L Account No. 2 | | | | |
|---|---|---|---|---|
| | Food | Liquor | Rooms | **TOTAL** |
| Sales | 200,000 | 200,000 | 200,000 | **600,000** |
| Purchases | 64,000 | 70,000 | 0 | **140,000** |
| **GROSS PROFIT** | | | | **460,000** |
| Wages | | | | |
| Kitchen | 76,000 | | | |
| Restaurant | 41,500 | 41,500 | | |
| Reservations/Check-in | | | 15,000 | |
| Housekeeping | | | 24,000 | |
| | | | | **198,000** |
| Direct Expenses | 29,000 | 29,000 | 29,000 | 87,000 |
| Overheads | 11,000 | 11,000 | 11,000 | **33,000** |
| **EBITDA** | -21,500 | 48,500 | 121,000 | **148,000** |
| EBITDA % | -11.0% | 24.5% | 60.5% | 30.0% |
| Depreciation | 10,000 | 10,000 | 10,000 | 30,000 |
| **EBIT** | -31,500 | 38500 | 111000 | **118,000** |
| | -16.0% | 19.3% | 55.0% | 19.6% |

# Appendix 3
# Initiative to convert a laundry room into a bedroom

**Assumptions**

We always fill the existing rooms every Friday, Saturday and Bank Holidays and at least one night during the week.

| Sales | | |
|---|---|---|
| | 1 room sold Friday & Saturday x 52 weeks of the year x £90 net of VAT | 9,360 |
| | 1 room sold midweek x 52 weeks of the year x £90 net of VAT | 4,680 |
| | I room sold each bank holiday x 8 | 720 |
| | SALES TOTAL | 14,760 |
| | Accommodation sales converted to EBITDA profit at 60.5% | |
| | EBITDA TOTAL | 8,930 |
| | Depreciation at 10% of cost | 2,000 |
| | Interest at 6.5% | 1,300 |
| | TOTAL ADDITIONAL PROFIT | 5,630 |
| Costs | | |
| | Bricks, mortar, fixtures, fittings and labour | 18,000 |
| | Disruption - 30 days of room next-door out of use | 2,000 |
| | TOTAL COST | 20,000 |
| ROI | % Return on Capital Investment | 28% |
| | Payback (approximate) | 4 years |

# Appendix 4 Causal Track

To show the effects of investment on profits, conversions, return on investment and net book value

| Year | 2017 | 2018 | 2019 | 2020 | 2021 |
|---|---|---|---|---|---|
| Capital Investment | 1,180,000 | 1,180,000 | 1,200,000 | 1,260,000 | 1,300,000 |
| **Initiatives Cost** | | | | | |
| 1. Creating a bedroom out of unused laundry room (opportunistic) | | 20,000 | | | |
| 2. Creating 3 new bedrooms out of managers flat (opportunistic) | | | 60,000 | | |
| 3. Refurbishment of toilets (Defensive) | | | | 20,000 | |
| 4. Create a new bedroom out of unused office (opportunistic) | | | | 20,000 | |
| 5. Other investment | | | | | |
| TOTAL NET BOOK VALUE | 1,180,000 | 1,200,000 | 1,260,000 | 1,300,000 | |
| **Sales** | 600,000 | 615,000 | 660,000 | 675,000 | |
| **EBIT Total** | 118,000 | 123,600 | 140,400 | 146,000 | |
| EBIT % | 20% | 20.50% | 23.20% | 24% | |
| **Return on Investment** | 10% | 10.30% | 11.10% | 11.20% | |
| **Sale/Purchase Value** using 10x EBIT multiplier | 1,180,000 | 1,236,000 | 1,404,000 | 1,460,000 | |

# What Customers Said

As we discussed our memories go back to your first year at the Sun in 2006. We called in one afternoon on our way home and instantly got a very nice feeling about the place. So much so that we booked our first stay with you very soon after.

It was at the time when you had started the renovation. We arrived and Lucy took us up to room 7. This was to become our favourite room on the many occasions we stayed there. At the time Lucy's Dad had been helping with his carpentry skills and had fitted either a new door or new door lock?

We settled into our room and relaxed before planning early doors in the bar. Eventually we decided to go down to the bar. It was then that we realised that the room door was stuck! We tried and tried to get out but it wouldn't budge. There wasn't any way to let Lucy know we were stuck so I had to think of another solution. I climbed out of the bedroom window and dropped into the church yard much to the amusement if passing tourists! I then walked into the bar to tell Lucy what had happened. To her credit she didn't flinch when I told her I had just dropped out of the bedroom window. She simply said "I'll get some butter"! We then returned to the room and after some strategic placing of the butter hey presto we were free!

(A remedy Lucy's Dad had recommended for stubborn locks)

It was the beginning of a 10 year relationship with room 7 and a place that became very special to us. So much so that with your help we married at St Mary's, had our wedding reception at the Sun Inn and stayed in room 7 as our honeymoon suite. A wedding reception that all our guests often refer to as the best wedding they ever attended. All thanks to you guys!

Chris and Julie

When Richard and I first met Mark and Lucy back in 2006 when they purchased The Sun Inn, it was with great relief that it soon became evident they understood exactly what our lovely old "local" needed in terms of not only refurbishment, but almost more importantly, the presence of very hands-on-ownership. And that is exactly what they delivered! Bringing the local community to its doors once again and providing us all with a lovely, sociable environment in which to meet friends. It was with great delight that we witnessed and enjoyed the huge improvements they made which were all very much in keeping with a traditional Inn in the heart of our lovely old market town.

On the subject of bells (most particularly on a Friday evening which was bell ringing practice) a person who shall remain nameless remarked whilst chatting with friends "Those b........ bells - they can get on your nerves sometimes". Our local Vicar overheard the remark, tapped him on the shoulder and replied quite rightly, "Those b...... bells have more right to be here than you have old chap!" which caused much merriment generally. All good fun.

Over the eleven or so years of Mark & Lucy's reign we continued to enjoy many social occasions in The Sun and in tribute to the new owners, Iain and Jenny, who have introduced subtle changes whilst retaining the original ethos, hope to continue to do so for many years to come.

Sue Bradshaw

Having stayed many times at the Sun Inn since the 1980s, Mark and Lucy taking charge in 2006 whetted our appetite to re-visit this characterful and charming 17th century coaching inn.

As it was our intention to acquire a cottage in Kirkby Lonsdale (only finally achieved in 2011), we took the opportunity to visit and stay over as often as our busy work schedules allowed. Even back in 2006, we were presented with so many accommodation and dining options in Kirkby Lonsdale, so why did we choose the Sun time and again? Well, the charm and character had already won us over many years earlier. What made the difference was the quality of the whole experience improving at each visit. Under Mark and Lucy's stewardship and through careful and sympathetic investment, the boutique style evolved with great rooms, superb en-suite facilities and top-quality Bath House toiletry products. I must also note the nice touches of home-baked biscuits and a delightful bottle of chilled fizz awaiting in our room. Moreover, under the then newly appointed Head Chef, the quality of the dining experience was further strengthened and this secured Mark and Lucy two AA Rosettes.

Above all though, our fond memories of Mark and Lucy's eleven-year tenure are shaped by the great team built around them, always happy to engage in amusing banter and providing a warm welcome together with excellent customer service. Moreover, in concluding, I cannot fail to mention Lucy's ability, whenever I phoned to book a room, to ensure our favourite Room Three was made available for us! As custodians of the Sun coaching inn for eleven years, you have indeed much to be proud of. We thank you!

Mike and Tom

Mark and Lucy would always go that little bit further to ensure that visitors received the total quality satisfaction package. An example of this comes to mind when one weekend we organised a reunion with four of our university friends. We all dined at the Sun and our friends stayed the night there. On returning home to Scotland one of the ladies realised that she had lost a small diamond earring. She contacted the Sun, among other places, in the hope that it was perhaps there that she had lost it. A couple of days later she was overjoyed when a small package containing the lost earring was delivered to her home, with compliments from Lucy at the Sun Inn, Kirkby Lonsdale.

After an exhaustive search It had been found in the bedroom. Our friend has never forgotten that.

Mark and Lucy were always professional, always caring."

Janet and Ty Power

Memories are the sweetest things,

They last from day to day,

They can't be lost, or cast aside,

And they can't be taken away.


How true is that? I hold some of my most treasured and happiest memories of 'The Sun Inn' that will stay with me, for all time.

A place where Dave, my husband, myself and often our family have celebrated some wonderful occasions.

...From enjoying delicious cuisine, on birthdays, anniversaries, parties and the entertaining of friends it had to be 'The Sun'... so it was the obvious choice for saying 'goodbye' to my much loved husband. 'The Sun' did this with great dignity and affection.

With Mark and Lucy at the helm, and their magnificent team, this well run establishment will always be remembered on my 'memory chart' - and I suspect on many other people's too.

Lynda Skinner

To contact Mark please send him an email at:

ringadingdingmark@outlook.com

Bar area

Bedroom used by staff

Shared guest bathroom

Clematis
Cottage
(above)

Our Wedding
(right)

Two views of the Bar area

Bar area

Guest room

Two views of the Dining room

Bar area

Restaurant

En suite bathroom

Guest room 3

Guest room 7

Guest room 12

Bedhead and side tables

Front door

Magazine rack

Panelling, the stool was upholstered by
Danny, another one of our treasured locals

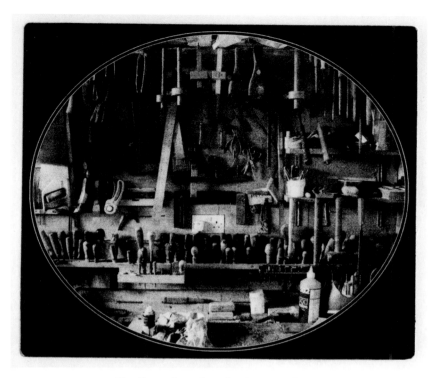

Dad's tools, taken by his son Peter

Tony & Eunice

Chefs: Sam, Angela, Luke,
Andy (Chopper), Alex

Sam & Shannon

Janine

Kev calling time, *Ring a Ding Ding*

Natalia

Steve